Margot Hellmiss

Natural Healing with
Cider Vinegar

Sterling Publishing Co., Inc.
New York

Library of Congress Cataloging-
in-Publication Data Available

10 9 8 7 6 5 4 3 2 1

Published 1998 by Sterling
Publishing Company, Inc.
387 Park Avenue South,
New York, N.Y. 10016
Originally published and © 1996 in
Germany by Südwest Verlag
under the title *Natürlich heilen mit
Apfelessig*
English translation © 1998 by
Sterling Publishing Co., Inc.
Distributed in Canada by
Sterling Publishing
%o Canadian Manda Group,
One Atlantic Avenue, Suite 105
Toronto, Ontario, Canada M6K 3E7
Distributed in Great Britain and
Europe by Cassell PLC
Wellington House, 125 Strand,
London WC2R 0BB, England
Distributed in Australia by
Capricorn Link (Australia) Pty Ltd.
P.O. Box 6651, Baulkham Hills,
Business Centre, NSW 2153,
Australia
*Manufactured in the United States
of America*

Sterling ISBN 0-8069-6167-8

Contents

*Almost all ancient cultures used
vinegar for healing purposes.*

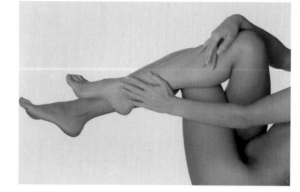

Using apple cider vinegar for tired, swollen legs.

Introduction

An old saying goes, "Sour makes us merry." People often used the saying to pacify children who didn't want to eat or drink sour fruits and juices. What seems at first glance to be a silly folk saying, is actually quite wise. We can see the wisdom in it when we take a closer look at the effect apple cider vinegar has on us. In truth, acidic foods can indeed lift our mood, refresh us, and free us from melancholy.

Apple cider vinegar contains many precious substances that stimulate the metabolism, improve blood circulation, and contribute to our general good health. One teaspoon (5 ml) of apple cider vinegar improves our well-being and puts us in a better frame of mind.

An Old Household Remedy

For a long time, people have used apple cider vinegar as a trusted household remedy. Our grandmothers and great-grandmothers knew that a beverage made with apple cider vinegar, water, and honey could help cure a variety of simple complaints.

This beverage decreases problems in the intestinal tract and with the metabolic process. It is an expectorant when you have a cold. In addition, it lowers cholesterol and is very helpful when you are trying to lose weight. Apple cider vinegar also has antibacterial and anti-inflammatory properties. In the past, these properties played a large role in treating wounds.

Used externally, apple cider vinegar is a natural skin lotion that helps establish the correct pH balance of the skin. People add apple cider vinegar to bath water and use it as a face lotion, a mouthwash, and a hair rinse. It is also helpful in treating cases of dandruff, leaving the hair shiny.

Today, many people have forgotten that vinegar is a disinfectant. In the past, before there was a pharmaceutical industry, vinegar played an important role in treating wounds.

Healthy Addition to Delicious Food

Apple cider vinegar is also a very delicate spice that should have a place in every health-conscious kitchen. It is excellent for improving salads, sauces, vegetables, and meat dishes. In Eastern European countries, people still use a beverage of apple cider vinegar and water as a refreshing thirst quencher.

In the past, people didn't rush to the doctor simply because they didn't feel well. Instead, they used apple cider vinegar as an all-around cure. Sometimes it even produced miraculous cures. People referred to it as "the fountain of youth" because they believed it prolonged the peak times of life and guaranteed a long life without the pain associated with aging.

Proven Remedy for a New Health-Consciousness

Today, we're very skeptical about stories of magical remedies. We know that they don't exist, just as no cure-all medicine exists. But apple cider vinegar has proven to be a natural, nutritious food that strengthens our health. Countless people have experienced its gentle healing power in different forms.

Folk medicine is a healing method based on experiences handed down over time. It is not based on scientific research. But science often confirms the effects of folk medicine. These are the same effects people have already observed over a long period of time. That apple cider vinegar contains valuable substances is no secret. We know that these substances have very beneficial effects on the human organism. Apple cider vinegar is an ideal substance today because people are emphasizing prevention, and apple cider vinegar is gentle and effective.

We can rely on the valuable experiences our ancestors had with this natural product. But why don't you check it out for yourself?

For years, fruit vinegar was the poor man's thirst quencher. But good cider vinegar, made from organically grown apples, is something rather special.

Nature's Apothecary

Our ancestors were very skilled in the use of natural remedies.

Scientific advances in the early twentieth century were one of the reasons many physicians took another look at medical ideas from the past.

Rediscovering Folk Medicine in Vermont

We credit Dr. D. Forest Clinton Jarvis (1881–1945) with rediscovering the healing properties of apple cider vinegar. He started his medical practice in Burlington, Vermont, specializing in problems of the ear, nose, and throat. Vermont is a state rich in forests. The Green Mountains, part of the Northern Appalachians, rise to an elevation of 4,400 feet (1,330 m). The state has a cool, temperate climate. Agriculture and the dairy industry are vital to its economy. In addition, many farmers also grow apples and make maple syrup.

This rough, isolated mountain region continued to leave its mark on the young physician. "I soon learned of the totally different ways people dealt with illnesses. I had to consider those ways seriously if I wanted to gain the trust of the local population." Dr. Jarvis came face-to-face with the folk medicine of the area, which he quickly realized "had little to do with what I had studied but which was an important part of life in Vermont."

Different Healing Methods

He learned about natural remedies made from leaves, herbs, and fruit whose uses were handed down from grandparents and great-grandparents. With the help of these remedies, people in Vermont successfully cured animals and people and effectively prevented many illnesses in the first place.

The methods used in folk medicine were simple, natural, and inexpensive. Many people continued to use them even after modern medicine was already in place. People in rural areas could not afford to see a doctor for every simple complaint. Often the doctor lived too far away, or the medicine was too expensive.

Old Traditions and the Modern Physician

Dr. Jarvis explored this "folk medicine" and discovered that simple, natural remedies are often better and work faster than conventional medicines. And despite the fact that he had grown up in this farm region, a place that taught him to love the earth and which had given him an innate sense of nature, it wasn't until he had been in practice for more than ten years that he finally understood this.

A Memorable Event

Dr. Jarvis recorded his experiences in manuscript form. Initially he intended this for his daughter and grandchildren. He wanted his descendants to know about these simple methods of staying active and healthy into old age. Finally, after much encouragement from his colleagues, he decided to make his studies of folk remedies available to a wider public. "I believe that the doctor of the future must not only be a physician but also a teacher. His true task will be to teach people how to live a healthy life. And physicians will not have less to do because of this; to the contrary, they will be even busier than they are today, because it is much more difficult to keep people healthy than to cure them of any illness."

The manuscript was published in book form in 1958. Within a few years, more than 500,000 copies were published and sold in twelve languages.

Today, medicine again accepts natural healing methods. But only a few decades ago, doctors ridiculed and attacked these methods.

Living 5 x 20 Years

In his book *Living 5 × 20 Years*, Dr. Jarvis talks about the close connection between life expectancy and nutrition. He discusses the surprising success that folk medicine in Vermont achieved with household basics, such as honey and apple cider vinegar.

Dr. Jarvis recommended a plain and simple recipe of water, apple cider vinegar, and honey specifically for prevention purposes. Used daily, the beverage lessens many complaints and prevents the development of illnesses.

Much of what we know about the effects of apple cider vinegar came from observing animals. For instance, he reports that when dairymen add fruit vinegar to cows' feed for a certain period of time, far fewer complications (such as inflammation of the udder, constipation, diarrhea, arthritis, colds, lung infections, etc.) occur. In addition, cows suffer fewer miscarriages, births are easier, and the calves are stronger and healthier.

He commented, "Those who know how to learn from bees, birds, cats, dogs, goats, calves, cows, steers, and horses will learn more about physiology and biochemistry than they find in any textbook."

> The more we know about the behavior of animals, the more astounded we are to learn of the logic they've used to adapt to their living conditions.

Clues from the Animals

Dr. Jarvis also discovered that under normal circumstances animals live five times the number of years they need "to reach maturity." For instance, a chicken is fully mature at six months and has an average life expectancy of about two and a half years. The life span of a horse that is fully mature at age four is twenty years.

On average, people are physically and mentally mature at twenty, so he considered a life span of one hundred years as absolutely normal, given sensible nutrition and life style. This is the meaning of the title of his book, *Living 5 × 20 Years*.

The Fundamentals of Folk Medicine

According to Dr. Jarvis, the roots of folk medicine in Vermont go back to the nomadic native population. They knew how to live in harmony with nature. These people observed animals and learned from them. They discovered that sick animals chewed very specific healing plants and herbs. They also observed that animals would not eat solid food when they were sick or injured. Instead, they only drank, and, to regain their strength, they isolated themselves from the herd, sought solitude and quiet, and moved around very little. In natural medicine, we would call this a healing fast. Dr. Jarvis said, "The roots of folk medicine go back to long-forgotten times. The first apothecary was Mother Nature."

Animals instinctively know what to do when they are ill or injured. Unfortunately, people are not even aware that they have this instinct.

Dr. D. Forest Clinton Jarvis rediscovered the healing power of apple cider vinegar in Vermont.

Prevention—Better Than Healing

Apple cider vinegar helps to correct deficiencies that are the result of poor nutrition. It supports natural body functions and is ideal for preventing illnesses.

Dr. Jarvis discovered that the main emphasis in folk medicine is on "the preservation of energy and health." In other words, the emphasis is on preventing illnesses from developing in the first place. Relieving complaints with simple and natural remedies is secondary.

According to folk medicine, illnesses do not develop spontaneously. Rather, they are the result of a continued and prolonged disregard for the fundamental rules of nutrition and of life.

How to Live to Be 100

Dr. Jarvis compared the body to a building which can only stay intact if the construction crews have used the best building materials. He felt that the "resistance and longevity of the building called the body depend on the food you eat, the liquids you drink, and the air you breathe." He believed that minerals play a particularly important role in maintaining good health.

For instance, without calcium we simply could not exist. Minerals support metabolism. They are indispensable in maintaining body structure and cell renewal, and they are helpful in defending against dangerous bacteria.

Apple cider vinegar contains all the beneficial minerals that are present in apples. And the honey, often added to apple cider, helps the minerals in the nectar and the natural sugars reach and strengthen the heart and circulatory system. In addition, our diet must include plenty of fruit, vegetables, and potatoes (carbohydrates), and it should be low in meat, eggs (protein), and fat.

Prevention: A Basic Recipe

❖ Mix a glass of water with 2 tsp. (10 ml) of apple cider vinegar and 1 to 2 tsp. (5 - 10 ml) of honey

❖ With small sips, drink this cocktail every morning.

In the introduction to his book, Dr. Jarvis concludes by adding, "More than anything else, folk medicine is attractive to people who refuse to accept a decline in physical strength as something unavoidable and who would much rather try to find a way to remain vigorous, active, and healthy to the end of their days."

Renaissance of Apple Cider Vinegar

Others versed in natural medicine have looked into the positive effects of apple cider vinegar. In 1949, Cyril Scott published *Cider Vinegar*, a small booklet on the subject.

In *The Great Book About Vinegar—Household Remedies from Grandmother's Times*, Emily Thacker talks excitedly about apple cider vinegar as "one of the healthiest, nutritionally richest liquids anywhere."

Later, Paul C. Bragg and Patricia Bragg recognized apple cider vinegar in *Health Elixir*. They felt that "pure, natural, non-distilled apple cider vinegar that is still cloudy is one of the most complete foods of nature."

In addition, countless collections of household remedies list apple cider vinegar as a gentle cure-all.

The use of apple cider vinegar to promote health is not a religion. But we know that those who pioneered its usage defend apple cider vinegar as a healthful remedy.

A Timely Remedy

Today, the pharmaceutical companies are producing more medications than ever before. Indeed, medicine today is capable of discovering, diagnosing, and treating illnesses which our ancestors were powerless against. But in spite of the great advances in the medical field, more and more people have noticed that often these expensive and lavishly produced salves, tablets, drugs, and drops do not lessen their complaints, and sometimes they produce a whole battery of undesired side effects.

A Variety of Effects

Today, we have a great amount of information available on health-related issues. Thus, we are learning more and more about the different options that can help us protect our health and help us heal. Consumers today are far more critical and health-conscious than they were in the past, and they are more aware of the risks and the undesired side effects of all treatments. So, why not practice prevention and use a natural remedy to deal with the first signs of an illness instead of "reaching for a cannon to kill a sparrow?" In fact, today, more and more people reach for the gentle remedies of nature.

The benefits of apple cider vinegar are widely recognized today, and natural, organically produced vinegar is now available everywhere. According to modern thinking, the most important key to our health resides in the food we eat. This knowledge is available to all who take responsibility for their health. For this reason, apple cider vinegar is experiencing a renaissance.

Apple cider vinegar is particularly beneficial because it can help cure a number of illnesses that are prevalent in modern societies.

What Apple Cider Vinegar Can Do

❖ It provides the body with essential minerals and trace elements, as well as calcium and a number of vitamins.

❖ It improves kidney function.

❖ It prevents the spread of harmful bacteria in the intestine.

❖ It improves tissues and keeps them supple.

❖ It improves blood circulation.

❖ It supports healing.

❖ It stimulates the metabolism.

❖ It strengthens the body's immune system.

❖ It detoxifies.

❖ It refreshes and revitalizes.

❖ It improves overall health.

❖ It delays the aging process.

A Short History of Vinegar

Apple picker (Roman mosaic from the third century A.D.).

Vinegar in Ancient Cultures

People began to make vinegar when they discovered that alcoholic beverages, such as wine, ferment and turn sour when exposed to the air. The Bible mentions apple wine and apple vinegar in several places. Egyptians, Syrians, Babylonians, Israelites, Greeks, Romans, and Germans all knew of vinegar and valued it as a way to give food a sour taste, to preserve meat, fish, and vegetables, and to quench thirst. They also valued it as a medicine. People used vinegar to tenderize meat and to cleanse stoneware. In fact, before people knew how to make wooden barrels, they made vinegar in stone vessels.

Vinegar in Antiquity

We know that around 5000 B.C., the Babylonians valued the healing properties of the vinegar that they made from the fruits of the date palm. They placed game in vinegar to prevent it from spoiling. One ancient Syrian manuscript mentions the use of vinegar compresses to treat ear pain.

The Phoenicians drank Shekar, a mild apple cider vinegar. They probably came upon this beverage by accident because they were unable to preserve apple wine.

In ancient times, people valued the healing properties of vinegar. They used it to disinfect wounds and to make compresses for

Cultures that knew how to make wine produced wine vinegar almost automatically. Juices, fruit wine, and apple cider vinegar developed in climates where people grew apples.

bruises and for insect bites and snake bites. They used vinegar diluted in water internally to lower fever, to speed wound healing, to improve digestion, and to cleanse internally.

Hannibal Took Vinegar on His Campaigns

Hannibal (247 to 183 B.C.), the great Carthaginian general, used vinegar to find an astounding solution to a problem.

Hugh rocks often blocked Hannibal's armies and elephants when they were crossing the Alps. Unlike horses, elephants cannot climb over high obstacles. Therefore, these rocks were insurmountable obstacles. The general came up with an ingenious idea. First he had his men build a fire around the rocks. When the rocks were sufficiently hot, his men poured vinegar over them. The vinegar "softened" the rocks, allowing the men to easily break them apart and clear them out of the way.

Cleopatra Used Vinegar to Win a Bet

Her contemporaries praised Queen Cleopatra for her beauty. Historians, however, admired her for the political cunning with which she manipulated the Roman Empire, a dangerous superpower.

The Egyptian queen Cleopatra (69 to 30 B.C.) loved to bet, on anything and everything. At one point, she won a bet by insisting that in a single meal she could eat the equivalent of one million in local currency. This was an unbelievable amount of money. It was unthinkable that one person could eat and drink that much in one sitting. But Cleopatra used a trick. She placed a string of pearls, worth one million in local currency, in a glass of vinegar. During the preparation for the feast, while the food was cooking, the pearls dissolved in the vinegar. At the beginning of the meal, the queen drank the "pearly" beverage and won the bet!

As an aside, ordinary Egyptians preferred a vinegary sour beer called Hequa, brewed from a type of rye.

As far back as ancient Egypt, women used apple cider vinegar as skin lotion. (Wall painting from around 1425 B.C.)

Posca—a Beverage Used by the Romans

The Romans produced vinegar from grapes, dates, figs, and from a specific brand of rye. The recipes survive in *De re rustica,* a book about agriculture and home economics written in 50 A.D. by Columella. When on a campaign, Roman legionnaires drank a mixture of vinegar and water every day. They used the mixture, called Posca, as a thirst quencher and as a disinfectant. It was a Roman legionnaire who took pity on Jesus Christ, hanging on the cross. Using a pole, he lifted a sponge saturated in vinegar water up to Jesus to relieve His thirst. According to the customs of that time, this was not additional torture, as many people assume today, but an act of compassion.

In ancient times, people used vinegar internally and externally for a variety of illnesses.

People in the Middle Ages Loved Tart Foods and Drinks

Within the past few years, supermarkets and grocery stores have offered an increasing variety of differently spiced vinegar.

During the Middle Ages, people used large amounts of vinegar and sour wine in their food. The acidity made fatty dishes easier to digest and prevented premature spoiling, which was particularly important in the absence of refrigerators and chemical substances to preserve food. In addition to apple cider vinegar, people also loved wine vinegar enhanced with elderberries, raspberries, orange blossoms, or rose buds. They also flavored vinegar with healing herbs and spices, such as anise, tarragon, cloves, and cinnamon. Of course, all of these gave the vinegar a pleasant fragrance.

Special street vendors, called vinegar runners, sold vinegar. Housewives would hand them containers to be filled. Women used vinegar to marinate cucumbers, cabbages, capers, melons, and even violets. At that time, vinegar was so popular that officials even taxed it.

A favorite beverage of the common man was a sour wine made from wild apples and spiced with sugar, rose water, and vinegar.

In recent years, people have become interested in the teachings of Hildegard von Bingen (1098–1179). She was well versed in the healing arts, including the use of apple cider vinegar to treat illnesses.

During the winter months, people made sour wine from wine or weak vinegar and spiced it heavily with mustard, cloves, sage, mint, parsley, ginger, pepper, cinnamon, and garlic. The abbot Antoine Furetiere, who wrote the *Dictionnaire universel*, listed sour wine and said that it is very good for the health if not kept too long.

Hildegard von Bingen (1098–1179), the famous scientist and mystic of the Middle Ages, was well versed in the healing arts. The natural recipes and healing methods she recommended are highly valued again today. Hildegard knew about the healing powers of vinegar. She recommended vinegar because of the beneficial effects it has on digestion. "Vinegar cleanses that which is smelly in human beings and makes sure that food takes its proper course."

When pestilence swept Europe, the physicians who treated the dying protected themselves against infection with vinegar. Because of its disinfecting properties, they also used vinegar to treat patients.

Vinegar for Health

Monsieur Maille was the royal merchant of vinegar and mustard at the French court. By 1750, he had a selection of fifty-five different types of vinegar, including a "vinegar for health" made with wild roses and chicory. French ladies frequently suffered bouts of fainting because of their tightly laced corsets, and they loved to add vinegar to their smelling salts. The vinegary aroma was helpful in recovering quickly.

The English poet Lord George Byron (1788–1824) lived for a time on only a beverage of vinegar and water and zwieback in order to lose weight.

During the nineteenth and twentieth centuries, people gave the healing effects of vinegar more emphasis. Some parents gave children vinegar water to quench their thirst. It was not as expensive as lemonade and was much healthier. Today, vinegar water is still one of the favorite thirst quenchers for people in rural Eastern Europe.

All members of society have used vinegar. The poor have used it as an inexpensive beverage, and the rich have used it as an exquisitely enhanced luxury product.

Vinegar comes in many different versions.

What Is Vinegar and How Is It Made?

The Work of Fermentation and Bacteria

Chemically speaking, vinegar is a watery solution of acetic acid, dye, and scented substances that are the natural consequence of acetic fermentation with bacteria.

Acetic Acid, a Strong Concentrate

Alkaline aluminum acetate is a compound formed from acetic acid. Highly diluted, this watery solution might be used to make a compress for bruises.

The basis of vinegar is acetic acid. It gives vinegar its sour taste and its preservative and antiseptic properties. Acetic acid (CH_3COOH) is fermented alcohol. But we can also produce it artificially with acetylene or by wood distillation. In its pure form or when it is too concentrated, acetic acid is highly corrosive. It is not uncommon for small children to be rushed to the hospital because they accidentally drank a twenty-five percent vinegar concentrate. In this concentrated form, we use acetic acid for cleaning and decalcification. In order to be used as a flavoring, the concentrate needs to be sufficiently diluted with water.

The Gentle Effects of Natural Vinegar

However, normal wine, herb, or fruit vinegar is completely different. As a rule, the acidity of natural vinegar is about five percent. At the most, it is seven percent. Diluted this way, acetic acid has a gentle, comforting effect and is never harmful, except to people who suffer from serious stomach illnesses.

The vinegar we routinely use in the kitchen (not a cheap blend made with synthetic acetic acid) is made through fermentation, more precisely through acetic fermentation. Whenever alcoholic beverages, such as wine, beer, fruit wine, or apple cider come in contact with acetic bacteria, they produce vinegar. These acetic bacteria are always present in the air and on plant material that is naturally undergoing fermentation. The bacteria react with the alcohol and combine with oxygen via enzymes. The result is acetic acid and water. As soon as the bacteria have finished their work, the alcohol in the liquid evaporates completely, and the alcohol content is less than one percent.

If you leave wine in an open bottle long enough (two weeks in the summer or four weeks in the winter), it will first turn sour and then become vinegar. Of course, manufacturers do not wait until fermentation concludes naturally. They add a specific, cultivated vinegar bacteria to speed up the process.

Making Apple Cider Vinegar

The basis of apple cider vinegar is apple cider, in other words, apple juice in which alcohol has developed. The greater the sugar content of the apple, the higher the alcohol content in the cider, and the easier it is for acetic acid to develop. Small aromatic cider apples make the best cider. If possible, you should place them in the cider press whole. If you only use discards or peels, stems, and pits, the quality is much poorer. Many people add yeast to the cider in order to increase the alcohol content. Often they also add special vinegar bacteria in order to speed up the development of acetic acid.

Of course, every producer has his own methods, and they often vary greatly. Some producers use apple wine they have stored in wooden barrels for years as a basis for their vinegar. Eventually, they ferment the wine in glass containers with specific vinegar bacteria cultures. Others use the Orleans or surface-fermentation

To make a particularly strong vinegar, use apples that are sweet and completely ripe. If you plan to make cider from the apples in your own garden, let them ripen on the tree.

process. This method dates back as early as the fourteenth century in the French town of Orleans. From manuscripts dating from the seventeenth century, we know that this is one of the oldest industrial production methods anywhere. The French laid oak barrels on their sides and filled them half full with apple cider. Eventually, they added a small amount of vinegar that introduced the bacteria. The air necessary for vinegar fermentation reached the apple cider through holes in the upper part of the barrel.

When the vinegar matured, they removed a portion and added fresh cider. This process continued until the barrels needed to be cleaned. To improve the aroma, they stored the finished vinegar in wooden barrels for a time.

Organically grown apples have not been exposed to artificial fertilizers or chemical herbicides. This assures the consumer that the product contains few, if any, dangerous substances.

It Must Be Naturally Cloudy

"Taste, enjoyment, and health!" That is what vinegar producers promise their customers. They make a point of letting us know that they make apple cider vinegar from sun-ripened apples grown in specially selected apple orchards. Their information often includes a guarantee that they used organic methods to grow their apples. Since the quality of the apple determines the quality of the apple cider vinegar, it goes without saying that producers use only the best apples with the least amount of environmental toxins. Of course, they only use whole apples. But just as important is how they make the apple cider vinegar. Some producers filter the apple cider vinegar too much or even

Choosing the Proper Vinegar

1. Buy only unfiltered, naturally fermented apple cider vinegar

2. Clear, distilled vinegar is missing many valuable substances

3. Make sure that the vinegar is made from organically grown apples. They assure the least possible presence of toxic substances.

distill it. The distillation process robs apple cider vinegar of important substances. Distilled vinegar has fewer vitamins, enzymes, minerals, and trace elements. Visually, the result is a clear vinegar with no foam on top.

Even if advertisements pander to our desire for beauty, and even if we might prefer something that is clear and pure for aesthetic reasons, we should not forget what is truly healthy. Natural apple cider vinegar, which has not been artificially treated, is infinitely more useful to our bodies and our health. A good-quality apple cider vinegar is dark and cloudy. It may have a foamy layer on top, and it may have a residue on the bottom.

"Mother of Vinegar"

"Mother of vinegar" is what we call the foam that floats on the top of apple cider or wine when it is about to turn into vinegar. The foam develops when the vinegar bacteria change ethyl alcohol into vinegar.

Two or three days into the fermentation process, a foam that looks like a spider web appears on the top of the cider. Producers remove this foam and add it to the next cider batch. Its speeds up the formation of acetic acid and gives the finished vinegar its specific aroma.

Some people insist that the layer of "mother of vinegar" is truly a magical remedy. They say that one spoonful reduces most of the complaints that also benefit from liquid vinegar.

However, "mother of vinegar" has a much more intense effect. It works particularly well for joint pain, infectious skin rashes, increased susceptibility to infectious diseases, and "unwelcome guests" in the intestinal tract.

The foamy layer that appears when vinegar is fermenting has nothing to do with mold. Unlike mold, this layer is digestible and very beneficial to our health.

A Well-Kept Secret from the Basement

Vinegar producers protect the "mother of vinegar" that comes from an expensive wine vinegar. They hand it down from generation to generation as a sacred secret. The specific vinegar bacteria transferred from one batch to the next batch consistently produces a vinegar with the same satisfying taste.

Of course, sometimes the "mother of vinegar" spoils. Then, it sinks to the bottom of the container. This happens when the container is disturbed, and the vinegar bacteria die because of a lack of oxygen. The "mother of vinegar" is useless and needs to be removed.

If you have no difficulty with food that has an unusual consistency, take a small spoonful of "mother of vinegar" and enjoy its effects. You can make "mother of vinegar" yourself at any time. All you need is fresh cider and vinegar. Pour equal parts of cider and vinegar into a container. Don't cover the container. After a few days, foam will develop on the surface of the liquid. However, if you store the container in a cool place, the process can take a few weeks.

Good apple cider vinegar depends on the quality of its basic ingredient. Only ripe, nutritious apples, free of pollution, are worth the effort to make your own apple cider vinegar.

How to Make Apple Cider Vinegar Yourself

You can usually find all the ingredients you'll need to make apple cider vinegar in any household. You need to keep the two steps separate. The first step is to make good-quality apple cider. The second step is to make the vinegar.

Use only sweet apples. If possible, use only those that have been organically grown. Pay less attention to the appearance. Be sure to avoid apples sprayed or grown with pesticides.

Commercial apple juice or apple cider, available in supermarkets, is not suitable for alcoholic fermentation because of the preservatives used.

Cider

❖ Wash and quarter approximately 10 lb. (4.5 kg) of apples.

❖ Use a juicer to make apple juice.

❖ Transfer the juice, including everything that remains in the juicer, into a larger glass or earthenware container. Dilute with a small amount of water. Add a pinch of yeast and a piece of dark bread to speed up the fermentation.

❖ Put a balloon over the opening to seal out the air. When the sugar in the juice changes to alcohol, the carbon dioxide which is created will slowly blow up the balloon. The foam on top usually comes from leftover yeast.

❖ Set the container aside for four weeks until all the sugar has changed into alcohol. After four weeks, the cider is finished. If the temperature is very warm, this process may only take one or two weeks. However, temperatures that are too high damage the cider. Yeast cells, naturally present on the outer skin of the apple, as well as those you add to the apple juice, die when the temperature goes above 140° F. (60° C). Without live yeast, fermentation is impossible. Cold temperatures also stop fermentation.

Apple cider is a refreshing, healthy beverage. But be careful, don't underestimate the amount of alcohol you are consuming.

Apple cider is known by many different names all over the world. Of course, it has different characteristics in each country. For instance, in France, people swear by the *cidre* they make from native apples. In Germany, people love the apple wine and apple cider of their region. Naturally, people believe that their cider and wine are special and much better than anything produced in any other region.

Vinegar

❖ Pour the apple cider into a wide, flat container that has a very large surface area. Fill the container three-quarters full.

❖ If you have apple cider vinegar or even some "mother of vinegar" on hand, add some to the liquid. This will speed up the fermentation. (Some vinegar producers also sell a special vinegar bacteria that you can use.)

The secret of many of the varieties of vinegar lies hidden in this unsightly mass of "mother of vinegar."

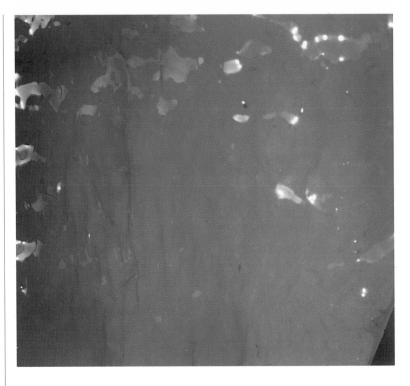

Vinegar eels (Anguilla aceti) are parasites which multiply in acidic substances.

❖ Cover the container with a linen cloth or mosquito net, but do not seal the container because vinegar bacteria need oxygen to do their work.

❖ The ideal temperature for fermentation is between 79° F. and 82° F. (26° C and 28° C). Above 95° F. (35° C), the bacteria die. If they are too cold, they simply stop working. As long as the bacteria are working, you might notice a smell somewhat like glue (ethyl acetate). However, as soon as the vinegar is finished, the smell disappears.

❖ After two to three months, the vinegar should be ready. Before you pour the vinegar into bottles, filter the liquid through a linen cloth. If you don't have one, a coffee filter will do. Filtering removes all the rough particles, pieces of apple, remnants of yeast, and the so-called vinegar eels.

❖ Pour the vinegar into bottles and close them with natural corks.

Don't be disappointed if your vinegar turns out too sour or doesn't taste quite right. Making good vinegar is an art, which a vintner or wine merchant will easily attest to. You'll need plenty of experience to do it well.

Nevertheless, making apple cider vinegar is much easier than, for instance, making balsamic wine vinegar, which takes twelve years or more to mature. No wonder a small bottle costs so much!

Determining Acidic Content

After you have gained some experience in making apple cider vinegar, you might want to know its acidic content.

Determining the exact amount, called titration, is quite a complicated process. Chemists use a specific substance as an indicator. This substance turns a particular color when acid is neutralized. First, you must add an exact amount of apple cider vinegar to this indicator. The indicator will show the typical acidic coloration. Next, you add an alkaline substance which neutralizes the solution. You need to record the precise amount of the alkaline substance you add. When the color of the indicator changes, the amount of alkaline substance used allows you to calculate the degree of acidity. However, this is a job for a laboratory because exact measurements are difficult with the tools most people have at home.

The other method is easy to use at home. Simply use a wine tester, which is available in specialty stores You can use the wine tester to analyze wine, and, with the help of a conversion table, you can also determine the acidic content of vinegar.

If you want to know if a liquid is acidic or alkaline, you can use litmus paper as an indicator. Litmus paper is blue and turns red when exposed to acid.

Apples are rich in healthy natural substances.

For centuries, people have observed and tested the beneficial effects of apple cider vinegar. Science, however, has still not figured out the details of why it is so beneficial.

What Makes Apple Cider Vinegar So Good for Us

Beneficial Substances

Almost everything we find in apples is also present in apple cider vinegar. For example, ½ cup (125 ml) of naturally cloudy apple cider vinegar made from whole apples contains the same amount of potassium as ½ cup (125 ml) of a fresh apple. Of course, a precise analysis of apples and apple cider vinegar varies somewhat because not all apple cider or all apples are the same.

A scientific examination of the substances in vinegar that evaporate shows how diverse the substances in apple cider vinegar are. Scientists measured ninety different substances, including thirteen carbolic acids, four aldehydes, twenty ketones, eighteen different kinds of alcohol, eight ethyl acetates, etc.

In addition, apple cider vinegar contains twenty important minerals and trace elements, acetic acid, propionic acid, lactic acid, citric acids, a number of enzymes, amino acids, and roughage (potash and apple pectin).

The Combination Is What Counts

What makes scientific evaluation so difficult is the fact that these substances interact with each other in diverse ways. In addition, they interact with substances from food and with substances found in the body itself. Scientists have not finished researching apple cider vinegar.

Apple Cider Vinegar for Healing

Experience, spanning decades and even centuries, leaves no doubt about the positive effects of apples and apple cider vinegar on the human organism. We even have a saying, "An apple a day keeps the doctor away." People who eat apples regularly or who drink apple cider vinegar are more vibrant, healthier, and have much smoother skin than those who don't.

The positive effects of most of the ingredients of apple cider vinegar have been clearly explained by science. This list includes a whole host of vitamins which are required for a well-functioning metabolism. It also includes apple pectin, which reduces cholesterol, and all of the minerals and trace elements, such as iron, copper, and fluorine, that serve as catalysts for the metabolism. Other ingredients, for example, potassium, calcium, magnesium, phosphorus, sulfur and chlorine, are critical for maintaining the structure of the body.

The secret is the combination. And that makes it difficult for artificially produced, isolated vitamins to have the same benefit as the vitamins contained in fruit, vegetables, or even apple cider vinegar.

Essential Substances in Apple Cider Vinegar

Minerals and Trace Elements	Vitamins
❖ Potassium	❖ Vitamin C
❖ Sodium	❖ Vitamin E
❖ Calcium	❖ Vitamin A
❖ Magnesium	❖ Vitamin B1
❖ Phosphorus	❖ Vitamin B2
❖ Chlorine	❖ Vitamin B6
❖ Sulfur	❖ Provitamin beta-carotene
❖ Copper	
❖ Iron	❖ Vitamin P
❖ Silicon	(a bioflavonoid)
❖ Fluorine	

Essential Potassium

Life would be impossible without potassium. Plants that do not have a sufficient amount of potassium die. When people have too little potassium, the vital activities in the cells diminish. Potassium regulates the water content in the cells, acting as a counterpart to sodium.

Cells are surrounded by a watery liquid which transports oxygen and nutrients into the cells and removes toxins and other waste products. This exchange between the liquid and the cells functions only when sufficient amounts of potassium are available. Taking toxins and waste products out of the cells is a cleansing process, greatly affecting the body's detoxification operation. If the potassium level is insufficient, the cells retain so much water that they eventually burst, damaging the surrounding tissue.

The results soon becomes obvious. The skin becomes weak and wrinkled, and muscles lose their firmness. This affects the compact muscle as well as the resilience of the blood vessels. Brain and nerve activities also depend on potassium. A potassium deficiency can cause exhaustion, poor memory, loss of appetite, and heart problems.

> Large amounts of potassium are present in the earth's crust. The daily requirement for an adult is 1,000 to 3,000 mg. A well-balanced diet will provide that amount.

Apple Cider Vinegar as a Source of Potassium

Since apple cider vinegar is a rich source of potassium, taking it on a regular basis often has astounding results for the problems mentioned above. Next time you are exhausted, try some apple cider vinegar and see if the reason for your exhaustion could be a lack of potassium. If so, you will not need coffee or any other stimulant to pep you up.

As an aside, the following foods are rich in potassium: lentils, beans, peas, marine algae, avocados, dates, and raisins.

Research done by J. Jagic in Austria has shown that eating apples on a regular basis can normalize blood pressure. The reason is that the potassium and other substances contained in apples help to withdraw excess water from the cells. Relieving water retention also removes excess sodium. Excess sodium is often the cause of high blood pressure in people who are sensitive to sodium.

Preventing Clogged Arteries

I invite you to try the eggshell test. Place a few eggshells in a glass jar of apple cider vinegar and close the lid. In a few days, the eggshells have dissolved, leaving behind only a thin membrane. The calcium in the apple cider vinegar dissolved the eggshells. There is a possibility that apple cider vinegar might dissolve, or at least reduce, calcium deposits inside human blood vessels in a similar way.

Calcium deposits develop primarily at the site of small injuries on the inside of arteries. These injuries are a byproduct of amino-acid metabolism. They reach the blood in greater amounts when we eat too much protein. Blood-clotting substances, such as cholesterol and calcium, cover the injured site. Over time, they can become so thick that they block the flow. This is a classic case of the body's own repair system going way beyond what it needs to do (healing injuries). Instead, it creates arteriosclerosis, a serious and sometimes fatal illness. However, as we saw with the eggshell experiment, apple cider vinegar may be able to break down the calcium and eventually dissolve it completely.

However, we don't know if this process can take place inside the arteries. After all, by the time the apple cider vinegar gets to the arteries, all the digestible components have been processed in the small intestine.

Apple cider vinegar prevents premature aging. Many reports also indicate that it prevents clogging of the arteries.

According to D.C. Jarvis, the founder of the therapy based on apple cider vinegar, possible deposits of calcium in the arteries eventually dissolve because of the natural acidity and the potassium in apple cider vinegar, which keeps arteries of free of calcium deposits.

Apple Pectin and Cholesterol

One thing is certain, apple cider vinegar and raw apples contain roughage called pectin. As is the case with all roughage, the body cannot digest pectin, so it helps keep digestion moving. Pectin has many other beneficial functions.

For instance, pectin is able to lower cholesterol, especially the dangerous LDL cholesterol. Pectin binds cholesterol that is made up of bile acids, which are essential and have to be available in order for the body to digest fat. The body draws cholesterol from the blood and changes it into bile acid. Pectin directly affects the condition of our blood vessels. If we have less cholesterol in the blood, less material will be deposited on the inside of the artery wall, and the flow of blood will increase considerably.

According to empirical studies, concentration, memory, vitality, body temperature, physical fitness, and all other functions that depend on improved blood circulation improve when you drink apple cider vinegar.

For a long time, people have used the pectin contained in apples to make marmalade and jams from fruit juices. Wouldn't it be interesting if this pectin could also be helpful in fighting high cholesterol.

The Pectin in Apples

❖ Pectin diminishes the risk of developing circulatory problems and premature calcification of the arteries.

❖ Pectin remains in the body longer than other roughage because it is water-soluble and not directly expelled from the body as is the case with fiber. In other words, pectin continues to work for a longer period of time than other roughage.

New Research Concerning Cholesterol

In 1991, University Hospital of Vienna published a study about the effects of apple pectin on the level of cholesterol in the blood. For six weeks, patients of various age groups, all with high levels of cholesterol, were treated with a roughage isolated from apple pectin. The result? The good cholesterol, HDL cholesterol, increased slightly, while the bad cholesterol, LDL cholesterol, which is responsible for slowing the flow of blood by calcifying the arteries, dropped by thirty percent.

Fighting Free Radicals with Beta-Carotene

Free radicals are aggressive substances that attack our cells. They are environmental poisons that enter our bodies when we inhale or when we eat. From a chemical point of view, free radicals have at least one unpaired electron in each molecule. In order to correct this deficiency, free-radical molecules pull electrons from within the cells, changing those into free radicals. This starts a chain reaction. The damage to the cells constitutes the first step in turning tissue rancid. Over time, such interference can lead to premature aging, problems in the immune system, heart problems, cataracts, and even cancer.

Dozens of scientific studies have proven that we can counteract the effects of free radicals with antioxidants such as beta-carotene. This substance, found in apple cider vinegar, is one of the most effective antioxidants.

In addition, the beta-carotene in apple cider vinegar is easier to digest than beta-carotene from other foods. A beverage of apple cider vinegar provides the beta-carotene necessary to defend the body from the damage that free radicals can cause. Because the primary source of free radicals is the polluted environment,

Due to increasing pollution in the environment, free radicals appear in ever greater numbers. For that reason, we must protect ourselves from them.

drinking apple cider vinegar regularly is even more important for us than it was for our grandparents.

As an aside, we might mention that the liver changes some beta-carotene into vitamin A, which is why beta-carotene is also called provitamin A.

Calcium: An Important Building Block

Of all the minerals in our body, calcium is the most abundant because it is necessary for bone and tooth development. The body only needs traces of other elements.

The skeleton of an adult person weighs about 11 lb. (5.5 kg). Approximately 2 lb. (1 kg) of that weight is calcium. A small amount of calcium is in muscle tissue, the blood, and other organs where it assures the efficient functioning of the muscles, nerves, heart, and assists with blood coagulation.

Calcium Sources in Your Diet

How much of the necessary amount of calcium is supplied by the food we eat depends on the "package" it comes in. For instance, foods such as spinach and rhubarb have an abundance of oxalic acid which interferes with the absorption of calcium in the intestines.

The most readily available calcium comes from milk and milk products. But that too creates a problem. With increasing age, many people develop an intolerance to lactose (milk sugar), which creates flatulence, diarrhea, and cramps. This intolerance eliminates one of the best sources of calcium.

Most older people get only half of the calcium their bodies need, even when they eat normally. That means they are only getting about 400 milligrams instead of the recommended 800 milligrams.

Broth made with beef bones is a rich source of calcium. However, widespread pollution in our environment has also affected the marrow in beef bones. In many instances, scientists have found lead in bone marrow. This leaches from the bones into the broth. In addition, doctors are not sure if mad cow disease, BSE, can be transmitted through bone marrow.

A calcium deficiency forces the body to withdraw calcium from the bones in order to use it for vital body functions.

The result? The bones become porous and thin, increasing the danger of fractures. Osteoporosis, with all its unpleasant manifestations, begins to develop.

Apple Cider Vinegar for Osteoporosis

One way of preventing this disease is to drink apple cider vinegar. It contains citric acid which makes it easy for the body to digest and absorb the calcium in the vinegar. In the same way, apple cider vinegar also increases the body's ability to absorb calcium from food.

By the way, adding a good bit of apple cider vinegar to a broth made with long marrow bones enriches the calcium content. Only 2 tbs. (30 ml) of apple cider vinegar added to 1 cup (250 ml) of broth greatly increases the calcium content of the broth, if you let it boil for up to two hours. After two hours, no additional calcium leaches from the bones.

Most physicians prescribe a calcium supplement for their patients to prevent or to treat osteoporosis. But the intestines don't absorb all supplements equally. To test the effectiveness of your supplement, try the test on this page. (from Emily Thacker)

Test Your Calcium Supplement

❖ Place one calcium tablet in 1 tsp. (5 ml) of apple cider vinegar.

❖ Allow the mixture to stand for about half an hour at normal room temperature, stirring every five minutes.

❖ If the tablet has not dissolved in the vinegar, your body probably cannot properly absorb the calcium. Switch to a different supplement.

❖ If your supplement passes the test, take the supplement with the apple cider vinegar you drink regularly. The combination will guarantee optimal absorption in the intestines.

Promoting Metabolism

The British-German bio-chemist Hans Adolf Krebs (1900–1981) proved the importance of vinegar acid for human metabolism in his research on the citric acid cycle.

Hans Adolf Krebs, who received the Nobel Prize for his 1953 discovery of the citric acid cycle in the human body, recognized that without acetic acid the metabolism would not function. Almost all metabolic processes produce an interim product called acetic acid. Without acetic acid, we would be unable to digest fat or carbohydrates, and the body would be unable to sustain life. A person needs up to 4 oz. (125 ml) of acetic acid for the metabolic processes to function properly.

Vinegar stimulates our metabolism. Drinking apple cider vinegar daily stimulates digestion and helps the body to absorb the fatty acids from food, making it easier for the body to convert carbohydrates (sugar and starch) into energy.

Vinegar Stimulates the Flow of Saliva

To ensure that a sufficient amount of acetic acid is available at all times, the body produces it. This means that the acetic acid in vinegar occurs naturally in the body.

We can see that vinegar effectively stimulates metabolism by examining the tongue. The sour taste of the acid literally creates a flow of water in the mouth, which means that the body is producing saliva.

Saliva plays an important function in the digestive process. More often than not, we underestimate this importance. Saliva's job is to liquefy food so that it can reach the intestinal tract easier. Saliva contains amylase, an enzyme which accelerates the breakdown of carbohydrates into their building blocks, the so-called simple sugars. The small intestines can only absorb carbohydrates in the form of simple sugars. The most important type of simple sugar is glucose. Without glucose we could not live. Glucose provides the energy the body needs to function. Those who take the time to chew food slowly and thoroughly, producing a sufficient amount of saliva, really do their bodies a great service.

And those who drink apple cider vinegar every day before each meal have what it takes for the body to make use of the carbohydrates in the bread, flour, potatoes, corn, or rice they eat.

Proper Amount of Cooking Salt

According to scientific research, too much cooking salt (sodium chloride) is harmful. One of the problems it creates is that the body retains too much water. In turn, this interferes with the detoxification process of the body and can, particularly in older people, elevate blood pressure to dangerous levels. But empirical evidence has shown that by drinking apple cider vinegar regularly over a period of two months, problems with aching joints can be helped. One possible explanation for aching joints might be a deficiency of minute doses of sodium chloride.

Of course we face a contradiction here. Most people eat too much cooking salt (the daily requirement is only a few grams), but they still complain about joint problems. Cyril Scott offers the following explanation for this contradiction "Salt in isolated form has completely different effects on the organism than the salt that is delivered by nature in a well-balanced combination with other minerals. For that reason, and as unbelievable as it may sound, a person can suffer from a salt deficiency even while consuming great amounts of cooking salt."

Too much of certain substances in the body can be just as dangerous as too little. It is important to provide substances in usable form and not disturb the physiological balance.

The Combination Is What Is Important

Scientific studies have identified many of the individual substances in apple cider vinegar. The key, however, is the way nature combines the minerals, trace elements, vitamins, and other substances in our food. The most efficient combination seems to be present in apple cider vinegar and in food seasoned with apple cider vinegar. Evidently, the salt we receive in this form is more beneficial than pure table salt.

Scientific studies have identified many substances that clearly have positive effects on the human organism. But science also confronts almost insolvable problems when interactions of these substances occur at the same time.

Spectacular Research Results

❖ The Medical Journal of Australia reports that vinegar is a proven first-aid treatment for jellyfish stings. Skin touched by the tentacles of the jellyfish is very painful. The patient can also suffer from nausea and other, more serious symptoms.

In Australia, more people die from the aftereffects of jellyfish stings than from shark attacks. Taking a little bottle of vinegar when going to the beach is a good idea in areas infested with jellyfish. Treat the skin immediately with undiluted vinegar.

❖ The latest research shows that apple cider vinegar contains a substance that is necessary for the growth of the placenta during pregnancy.

Scientists have not yet identified the characteristics of this substance. Thus, we could be dealing with an unknown vitamin.

In any case, this might explain why pregnant women often crave sour food.

❖ According to a study conducted by Ancel Keys, eating one apple before going to bed keeps the level of blood sugar constant, assuring a good night's sleep.

❖ Many physicians recommend that swimmers who frequently suffer from ear infections flush the ear with a mixture of boiled water and vinegar. This disinfects the ear, preventing infection.

❖ The Japanese Journal of Pharmacology stated that vinegar might be used to prevent stomach ulcers that are the result of alcohol abuse.

Even though scientists are still doing research, many people believe that vinegar stimulates the production of gastric juices that protect the stomach lining from being damaged by alcohol.

Preserving Food with Vinegar

Preserving Food the Natural Way

Using cold temperatures is one of the oldest methods for preserving food. From the Neanderthals on, our ancestors kept their game fresh by keeping it in cold caves and by allowing it to freeze during the winter. Cold anesthetizes microorganisms, preventing them from doing their destructive work. This is particularly true of bacteria or mold spores. If temperatures are low enough, these microorganisms will die. Today we use a freezer.

Vinegar Kills Germs

Like cold temperatures, vinegar also kills mold and decay-causing microorganisms. The acidity of vinegar increases the acid content of the food being preserved which kills microorganisms, germs, and spores. Many of these organisms require a finely tuned balance between acidity and alkalinity and cannot survive in the presence of vinegar because of its acidity.

D.C. Jarvis has illustrated this with the following test. He placed an earthworm, which is very similar to the parasites in the intestines and in spoiled food, in vinegar. "In a few seconds, vinegar had destroyed its life." In much the same way, fruit vinegar kills dangerous bacteria in our intestinal system. It also kills bacteria and other microorganisms that spoil food.

By the way, it is not just the vinegar's acidity that preserves food; the tannin present in apples is also a preservative. In addition, apple cider vinegar contains propionic acid which has preserving characteristics.

Many scientific tests have proven that apple cider vinegar is a preservative, but people who have used apple cider vinegar have known this for a long time. Under normal conditions, cucumbers preserved in vinegar will keep for months. Under the best conditions, in a tightly closed container, they will keep for a few years.

Crushing an apple to make juice or cider releases tannin, a natural preservative within the cells. When exposed to air, tannin gives sliced apples and apple juice their golden yellow color.

Three Preserving Substances Found in Apple Cider Vinegar

❖ Vinegar acid   ❖ Tannin   ❖ Propionic acid

Preserving with Vinegar

Apple cider vinegar contains propionic acid which preserves food. It can be produced artificially. We use this substance to preserve food for humans and for animals.

Preserving food with vinegar is so simple that you, too, should try it. You can guarantee your own personal flavor, and you will know that the food you have preserved does not contain any artificial preservatives.

❖ Make sure you use only the freshest vegetables. The following work particularly well: cucumbers, onions, miniature corn on the cob, beans, cauliflower, Brussels sprouts, asparagus, carrots, shallots, mushrooms, and eggplant.

❖ Wash, clean, and chop the vegetables. Slice the carrots, mushrooms, and green beans in half. Cut cauliflower in small portions, etc.

❖ Cook the vegetables in the usual manner, adding a small amount of salt to the water. When they are finished, rinse them in ice-cold water. Cut the cucumbers in half or slice and layer them in a container. Season each layer to your taste or sprinkle with salt, but be sure to use the salt specifically intended for canning food since it has no iodine or any other additives that would discolor the food. Cover the cucumbers with water and allow them to soak overnight. Drain the water the next morning.

❖ Place the vegetables in alternating layers in a glass jar with a screw-on lid.

❖ Add vinegar to the salt water in which you boil the vegetable. You may also want to add wine, sugar, and spices. Allow the liquid to come to a boil quickly. Sugar also has preserving properties and lessens the tartness of the vinegar. You may use any of the following spices: mustard seeds, garlic, basil, dill, oregano, horseradish, tarragon, bay leaves, cloves, or peppercorns.

❖ Pour the hot marinade over the vegetables in the glass jar. Screw on the lids and allow the glasses to rest upside down on the lid for about five minutes. Then you have to wait three weeks until you can taste your creation!

Vinegar Disinfects

The reason vinegar is so beneficial for preserving food is that it kills the bacteria and other microorganisms that will spoil stored food. Vinegar also destroys a string of microscopic, illness-causing bacteria that can affect the skin, throat, lungs, bladder, and intestines. More than 2,500 years ago, the Greek physician Hippocrates used vinegar to treat wounds and intestinal infections because of its infection-fighting properties. In the past, soldiers have placed a vinegar-soaked cloth on their injuries to prevent "wound fever."

Vinegar is an also an antiseptic. This means that the vinegar's acidity renders many types of bacteria, viruses, and other germs harmless. And, in addition, vinegar is an antibiotic. Specific bacteria in vinegar attack and kill a whole host of illness-causing agents.

Of course vinegar also has its limitations. It is ineffective against serious infectious diseases, such as typhus, measles, or malaria. On the other hand, we have no evidence to prove how effective vinegar could be if used prior to the onset of such illnesses.

We have reports that there really were "vinegar thieves" in Europe during the time of the plague. These were people who rubbed vinegar over their entire bodies so that they could break into the houses of the sick or those who had just died from the illness. Of course, we cannot prove that they really had protected themselves from being infected. The fact remains that they knew, perhaps from experience, how to protect themselves against the Black Death.

Throughout time, people have known about the disinfecting properties of vinegar. People have used it to clean dishes, kitchen boards, stoves, garbage cans, furniture, toilets, laundry, and much more. They knew that it worked and that it killed many germs in the process.

Prevention and Treatment with Vinegar

❖ Sore throat (gargle)

❖ Ear infection (rinse ear canal, steam bath)

❖ Throat infection (gargle)

❖ Colds (vinegar compresses on the chest)

❖ Infected gums (gargle)

❖ Wounds (take orally and apply externally)

❖ Kidney or bladder infection (take internally)

❖ Body odor (apply externally)

❖ Nervous cough (inhale or place a few drops on your pillow)

❖ Skin infection (apply externally)

❖ Light intestinal infection (take orally)

❖ Athlete's foot (apply externally and wash socks in vinegar)

❖ Itching hemorrhoids (dab with a cloth soaked in vinegar)

Fighting Intestinal Poison with Vinegar

We cannot overestimate the ability of vinegar to kill bacteria. Indeed, as far as our health is concerned, this may be vinegar's most important characteristic. In the same way that food will rot when it comes in contact with bacteria, the food we eat can also literally rot in the intestines. The bacteria that are responsible for this flourish in an unhealthy intestinal tract.

Tracing Intestinal Problems

Many of us feel that this does not apply to us because our digestion is perfectly normal. But we could be wrong. Even occasional constipation, diarrhea, flatulence, stomachache, irregularity, unusually formed, or foul-smelling stool is an indication that something is not quite right.

We usually don't discuss our intestinal problems. But today's hectic life and unhealthy diets contribute a great deal to these problems. Unfortunately, more and more people are trying to deal with intestinal problems.

We can trace a whole host of small complaints, and often more serious ones, back to unhealthy conditions in the intestinal tract, even though the complaints don't seem to have anything to do with digestive problems. Here are some examples: skin problems such as acne or boils, excessive sweating, mucus in the eyes, styes, bladder problems, headaches, inflamed joints, gout, sciatica, depression, and many others. All of these can point to an insidious process of toxins originating in the intestines.

If the digestive system is regularly under stress, then over time, the walls of the intestine will become sluggish. Movement of the contents of the intestines slows down, and stubborn deposits accumulate in the countless folds that line the inside of the intestine. Since the intestines, with all their convolutions, are approximately 20 feet (6 m) long, a considerable amount of "intestinal garbage," as F.X. Mayr called it, accumulates. Mayr was a physician who specialized in treating disorders of the intestinal tract.

This "intestinal garbage" is a true paradise for bacteria. They promote fermentation toxins, such as methanol, butonal, and other gases that simply put us in a bad mood. Later, they can slowly poison the whole system.

Eating too much at one sitting, eating too often, or eating a large meal late in the day can tax the intestinal system. Processed foods, such as sweets, bleached flour, and alcohol, lack natural roughage and contribute to intestinal stress.

Regulating Digestion Naturally

Taking apple cider vinegar on a regular basis can counteract the process described above in several ways. Vinegar attacks bacteria as well as other harmful intestinal parasites. Many people who drink vinegar water regularly notice a decrease in flatulence and a less unpleasant smell of their stool within a few days. These are indications that the apple cider vinegar has reduced the poisonous substances in the intestinal tract and created a much healthier environment. Drinking apple cider vinegar and water also reduces feelings of hunger. Furthermore, vinegar stimulates the metabolism and the production of digestive enzymes. Apple cider vinegar has no side effects and can prevent intestinal stress, which can have serious health consequences.

*Honey and apple
vinegar are ideal partners*

ple Cider Vinegar
a Remedy

Apple Cider Vinegar and Honey, the Elixir for Health

Apple cider vinegar and honey make a perfect pair. Honey reduces the tartness of the vinegar and is rich in vitamins, minerals, trace elements, enzymes, and antibacterial substances. Many conditions, such as intestinal problems, colds, coughs, and exhaustion, for which apple cider vinegar is recommended also react favorably to honey. What could be more logical than using them together?

For general health and a long life, D.C. Jarvis recommended that people drink a mixture of water, honey, and apple cider vinegar every day. The proportions for this are 2 tsp (10 ml) of apple cider vinegar and 2 tsp. (10 ml) of honey in a glass of water. Dr. Jarvis considered honey to be "a truly complete food." He recommended it for healing purposes, as a sleeping remedy, for coughs, burns, illnesses of the respiratory tract, sinus infections, hay fever, and muscle cramps. Because honey supports health and kills germs, each glass of apple cider vinegar and honey is a perfect prescription for health.

A few manufacturers of apple cider vinegar offer a mixture of apple cider and honey. This is often called a "power drink."

The Antibacterial Effects of Honey

Honey contains all the substances found in the natural nectar of flowers. We also find vitamin C, several B vitamins, amino acid, and citric acid, as well as minerals such as potassium, calcium, iron, copper, manganese, phosphorus, and magnesium. Some of the substances contained in honey act as inhibitors that render bacteria harmless.

In particular, the potassium in honey kills bacteria. Potassium dehydrates and literally dries out the bacteria. If, for instance, we place the bacteria that cause typhus, dysentery, intestinal disorders, or lung infections on pure honey, the bacteria will die within hours or, at the latest, within a few days.

This does not mean that honey can cure illnesses caused by these bacteria. In fact, these illnesses are serious and, in general, require strong medication. But the bacteria-killing properties of honey have been proven and can protect our bodies from many troublesome and even dangerous germs.

All honey produced in Germany is natural and free of additives. In 1976, the country passed a law which made it illegal to add any artificial substances to honey.

Naturally Pure Honey—Provider of Energy

❖ The basic substance of honey is nectar from flowers. Nectar is primarily sugar, and except for starch (a complex sugar), sugar is the most important provider of energy. In two words, it is pure energy. However, in order for sugar to be used by the body, digestive enzymes must first change natural sugar (sucrose) into simple sugar (fructose and glucose).

❖ In the case of honey, this change to simple sugar has already taken place. When bees collect nectar, specific enzymes in their stomachs change the sugar in the nectar to fructose and glucose. We could say that the bees have taken over part of the work of our digestive system, which is why honey is so easy to digest.

❖ The body directly absorbs the energy provided by honey. You can experience this by taking a spoonful of honey when you are exhausted. In only a few minutes, you'll feel refreshed, and you'll have more energy.

Honey: Provider of Vitamins

To metabolize sugar, the body requires an array of vitamins and other substances that are present in honey. This distinguishes honey from so-called empty carbohydrates, such as refined sugar. The body takes the vitamins necessary to digest refined sugar from food and places where the vitamins are stored. This makes refined sugar, in contrast to honey, a vitamin thief.

Honey in Asian Medicine

People in Asia have always considered honey a complete food and an effective remedy. In Tibet, they treat all complaints that include severe mucous congestion with a diet that includes large

People believe that the prophet Mohammed drank a glass of water with honey first thing every morning. He said: "When a person eats honey, a thousand remedies enter his stomach, while one million illnesses will leave."

Natural medicine knows how beneficial and healing honey and apple cider vinegar are for the stomach and intestinal tract. The combination helps prevent constipation, diarrhea, and other intestinal problems.

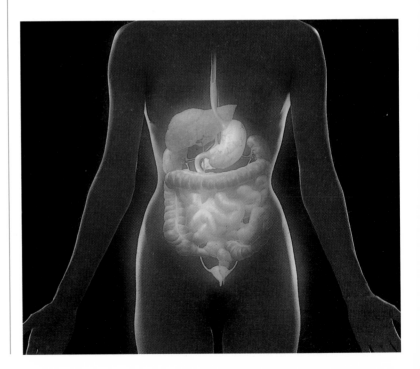

amounts of honey and sour, but light drinks. Obviously, drinks combining apple cider vinegar and honey fulfill these requirements.

For the Respiratory Tract and Digestion

According to Ayurveda, an ancient Indian form of medicine, people who have a cough, bronchitis, or a cold should drink hot milk with honey. Chinese medicine, too, trusted honey for such complaints, particularly when the patient had a constantly running nose. In case of constipation, Chinese medicine recommended 2 tsp. (10 ml) of honey in a glass of boiled water. Sufi healers in the Middle East recommend hot honey water in cases of diarrhea. In Japan and China, people with intestinal flu are given fresh honey three times daily, before each meal. Ayurvedic medicine also considers honey as an aid to mental clarity and suggests taking a teaspoon (5 ml) of honey with kalmus root powder in the morning and evening to combat forgetfulness and a lack of concentration.

Natural science can easily explain the effectiveness of all these treatment methods, many thousands of years old. Their effectiveness is based on the fact that honey effectively kills bacteria and provides energy.

Honey is only valuable if it has not been heated above 140° F. (60° C). Make sure that the label of the honey you buy says "cold pressed" or "rich in enzymes." Manufacturers of quality honey use a special selection process, carefully handling the honey. But even the best honey will suffer in quality when used in cooking or baking, when heated in the kitchen, or when stored in the refrigerator.

What Apple Cider Vinegar Can and Cannot Do

Apple cider vinegar is an ancient and effective house remedy in folk medicine. In folk medicine, the primary objective is prevention, protecting the organism from becoming a breeding ground for the bacteria that cause illnesses. Apple cider vinegar, the cloudy, tart liquid that even children like to drink, contributes to keeping the body healthy when combined with a balanced diet and an active lifestyle. Protected this way, the body is capable of defending itself against illnesses.

According to Cyril Scott, one of the many who believed in healing with apple cider vinegar, "Apple cider vinegar is not a cure for any specific illnesses but its role is to increase health."

We can use apple cider vinegar to help treat a host of simple complaints such as cough, hoarseness, constipation, and heartburn. For minor discomfort, or when feeling unwell, we suggest you try this proven house remedy. We can second Cyril Scott's statement that apple cider vinegar "is useful for a whole host of different situations without causing harmful side effects."

On the other hand, apple cider vinegar cannot perform miracles. Most certainly it is not a medication that you should prescribe for yourself for chronic problems or for serious illnesses. These should always be treated by a physician. We would like to emphasize that you must refrain from treating yourself with house remedies when you have serious complaints or when you are unsure of a situation. However, after consulting with your physician, you may continue to use apple cider vinegar as a supplement to other medical treatments.

Uses

You can use apple cider vinegar mixed with water for gargling, inhalation, as a hair rinse, or for massaging the skin. You'll find when to do what in "Uses from A to Z," page 49 and "Apple Cider Vinegar for Hygiene," page 76.

In many instances, apple cider vinegar is taken as a beverage. Use it regularly for at least four weeks in order to experience the benefits.

As a general conditioning treatment, drink apple cider vinegar in water every morning for at least six to eight weeks. Follow the basic recipe. This requires only a small amount of effort, and soon you won't want to be without this revitalizing drink. To improve the overall state of your health, make this a habit for the rest of your life.

Basic Recipe

Use 2 tsp. (10 ml) of apple cider vinegar to a glass of water. Adding 1 to 2 tsp.(5–10 ml) of honey is optional. Mix well, drink slowly, and enjoy.

As a general support for your health, drink this mixture before breakfast. Some people may want to drink an additional glass with lunch and dinner. In the words of D.C. Jarvis, "In this way you will receive the acidity that the fruit, leaves, and roots have gathered from the soil. This beverage is an excellent strengthening supplement that can be taken before, during, or after a meal."

Variations

People who can't take this beverage on an empty stomach should drink it after breakfast. The addition of honey will make it easier on the stomach. You should experiment to find the right dose for you, depending on how it tastes and how well you tolerate it. While some people only add 1 tsp. (5 ml) of apple cider vinegar to a glass of water, others add a healthy portion.

This cocktail tastes good, much like tart apple juice. You may also mix the apple cider vinegar with vegetable, tomato, or apple juice or add it to any other cold drink. Experiment and see what you like best!

Many people call apple cider vinegar "the fountain of youth" and "a magical health elixir." They praise it as an all-around cure for a variety of complaints. But why exaggerate? Instead, why not report its obvious benefits.

Use Apple Cider Vinegar with Care

❖ While scientific research has identified individual substances in apple cider vinegar, no large studies or double-blind studies have tested the effectiveness of apple cider vinegar.

❖ Should you discover that apple cider vinegar does not agree with you, try to find other ways to increase your health and well-being. Pay attention to your needs. What is beneficial for many is not necessarily beneficial for all.

❖ Please remember that folk medicine is the result of experience. The effectiveness of many of the healing methods discussed here has not been scientifically researched yet.

Do You Need Apple Cider Vinegar?

	Yes	No
Do you suffer from sluggish intestines (feeling of fullness, diarrhea, constipation, nausea)?	❐	❐
Do you tend to be depressed?	❐	❐
Do you have frequent headaches?	❐	❐
Do you have joint pains?	❐	❐
Are you nervous and tend to have a sharp tongue?	❐	❐
Are you prone to infectious diseases?	❐	❐
Do you get colds frequently?	❐	❐
Do you tire easily?	❐	❐
Is your hair dull?	❐	❐
Do you lose a lot of hair?	❐	❐
Do your fingernails break easily?	❐	❐
Do your scratches and cuts heal very slowly?	❐	❐
Does your scalp or skin itch frequently?	❐	❐
Have you noticed that you have more calluses or corns?	❐	❐
Are your feet and hands cold, or do you often feel cold?	❐	❐
Does it seem as if your memory and concentration have decreased noticeably?	❐	❐
Do you always go shopping with a list because otherwise you would forget half of what you need?	❐	❐
Is it becoming increasingly difficult to make decisions?	❐	❐
Do your eyes tire easily?	❐	❐
Does food not taste as good as it used to?	❐	❐
Do you get out of breath at the slightest exertion?	❐	❐
Do you have a lot of cavities or gum infections?	❐	❐
Do you have bad skin?	❐	❐
Do you sometimes wake up at night because your arms or legs have fallen asleep?	❐	❐
Do you have difficulty falling asleep or sleeping through the night?	❐	❐
Do you have difficulty unwinding?	❐	❐
Have you noticed that sometimes your eyelids flutter or twitch uncontrollably?	❐	❐

Uses from A to Z

Premature Signs of Aging

If you think that you have been aging more than you should, try to determine why your body is not regenerating itself properly. Using a treatment of 2 tsp. (10 ml) of apple cider vinegar and 2 tsp. (10 ml) of honey in a glass of water every morning over a longer period of time often solves the problem.

Increasing body fat, hair loss, deteriorating teeth, poor memory, hearing problems, eyes that tire quickly, creaking and painful joints, discolored fingernails, and age spots on your hands are not inevitable signs of advancing age as many people assume. Rather these are all signs that "your metabolism and the internal balance of your system is disturbed," as Cyril Scott stated. These are signs of a body that needs support so it can regenerate itself.

When these signals appear, don't stand idly by, resigning yourself to getting old. Fight this premature wear and tear by consciously making healthy choices.

In many instances, apple cider vinegar, a healthy diet, and an active lifestyle can improve these conditions and slow down the aging process.

Effect: Improves circulation, detoxifies, revitalizes, and provides minerals.

Athlete's Foot

To rid yourself of athlete's foot, dab the affected area with undiluted apple cider vinegar several times during the day and in the evening before going to bed. You must wear socks made of natural fiber. At the end of the day, soak the socks in vinegar water for half an hour before washing them.

Effect: Kills germs.

weakness

... ɔ have the urge to urinate in the middle of the night
... ık apple cider vinegar before each meal until the urge
... Bladder infections also react favorably to this cocktail,
... ı supplement to medical treatment.
... rmalizes urine that is too acidic or too alkaline and
... ney function.

... ɔblems

You can also lessen breathing difficulties by saturating gauze bandages in apple cider vinegar and wrapping them around your wrists.

If you have breathing problems or wake up during the night because of breathing difficulties, try drinking a glass of water with apple cider vinegar and honey. Drink it in small sips or by the teaspoon (5 ml) so that it takes approximately thirty minutes to drink it all. Then, wait for a while and see if your breathing has become easier. If not, repeat the procedure.

People have reported that this beverage is also helpful in cases of asthma, but only in addition to medical treatment.

Effect: Calms and relieves cramps.

Bruises

... mpress made of apple cider vinegar and salt dissolves black
... marks relatively quickly.
... .ions: Heat ¼ cup (62.5 ml) of apple cider vinegar with
... (7.5 ml) of salt. Saturate a cloth and place it on the affect-
... t. Repeat the procedure when the cloth begins to dry.
... ect: Reduces swelling.

To Avoid Burping

❖ Eat slowly and chew thoroughly.

❖ Eat several small meals throughout the day rather than a few large ones.

❖ Try to avoid foods that are difficult to digest, such as legumes, fried foods, and foods that are very sweet, salty, or highly spiced.

❖ Skip dinner or eat oatmeal or a dry roll instead.

Burns

According to an old home recipe, you should immediately treat light burns with vinegar water.

Effect: Cooling and disinfecting.

Burping

Burping is a sudden rising of air or other sour-tasting matter from the stomach through the esophagus and into the mouth. In some ways, it is a normal side effect of digestion. If it is too pronounced and causes discomfort, try apple cider vinegar. Drinking it with water at each meal can prevent burping.

Effect: Balances stomach juices.

Colds

When you have a cold and stuffy nose, inhale the steam produced by diluted apple cider vinegar and watch how quickly you can breathe again. And if your nose isn't completely clear, at least you will notice some relief. This steam is very healing and has no side effects. If the steam bath is not effective, repeat the process, several times if need be. In addition, drink apple cider vinegar and honey in water once or twice daily. You should also drink this cocktail if your sinuses are clogged or if mucus is dripping down your throat.

To prevent frequent colds, particularly during the cold season, visit a sauna regularly. The steam strengthens your immune system and your resistance.

Effects: Reduces inflammation, loosens mucus, and is antibacterial.

People who suffer from poor circulation or have a constantly red or runny nose due to a cold should give the following home remedy a try.

❖ Mix 1 cup (250 ml) of warm water with 3 to 4 tbs. (45 - 60 ml) of apple cider vinegar.

❖ Dip a piece of cotton in the liquid and dab the sore areas around the nose for five minutes.

❖ Repeat the application several times a day.

Colds and Slight Fever

For generations, people have used their grandmother's recipes faithfully, even if they seemed slightly amusing. But a lot of these healing remedies can indeed be beneficial. Sometimes all we need to do is experiment.

Always try to discover the cause of a fever because sometimes more is involved than simply a harmless cold.

Pepper and Apple Cider Vinegar on Paper

According to an ancient household recipe, you can fight a cold by soaking a piece of brown wrapping paper, about 8 inches (20 cm) square, in apple cider vinegar. As soon as the paper is saturated, sprinkle it with a little bit of pepper. Place the paper on your chest, holding it in place with a bandage wrapped around your chest. Remove the bandage and paper after 20 minutes and wash the skin. Be careful not to get chilled.

Lower Leg Compresses

Lower leg compresses that use vinegar water are not all that strange. They have been proven to lower fever that is associated with a cold. Physicians often recommend these compresses. However, you should only apply them when the patient is comfortably warm.

Directions: Mix 3 cups (750 ml) of water with 1 cup (250 ml) of fruit vinegar. Soak two linen towels in the solution. Wring out the excess liquid and wrap the cloth around each calf. Cover the lower legs with towels. Keep the patient nice and warm with blankets. As soon as the compresses are dry, repeat the process.

Vinegar Socks

Vinegar compresses on the feet reduce fever.

Directions: Soak a pair of cotton socks in vinegar water. Wring out the excess and pull the socks over the feet. Wrap each foot in a towel and rest. Make sure the patient is comfortably warm. In case of high fever, soak the socks in pure apple cider vinegar.

Effect: Reduces fever.

Cough

Coughing often afflicts children. In the past, people called the doctor immediately. However, folk medicine recommends apple cider vinegar as an effective home remedy for light coughs. This remedy also works well for a throat irritation that keeps hanging on after a cold.

Directions: Mix ½ cup (125 ml) of honey with 3 to 4 tbs. (45 - 60 ml) of apple cider vinegar.

❖ Take 1 tbs. (15 ml) of this mixture during a coughing fit or 6 tbs. (90 ml) spread over the whole day. Stir well before each use.

❖ Take 1 tbs. (15 ml) before going to bed; in addition, take 1 tbs.(15 ml) should you wake up during the night.

Effect: Dissolves mucus, relaxes, calms, and reduces inflammation.

Here is another old home recipe for people frequently plagued by coughs. Put a few drops of apple cider vinegar on a cloth placed on the pillow. You may also place a piece of cloth soaked in apple cider vinegar on your head.

Detoxification

For people who are fasting or using a detoxification treatment, we highly recommend a glass of apple cider and honey in water every

Gargling with apple
vinegar in water
fight bad bre
are fasting
coating

Detoxification

❖ Fast for two days, taking no solid food.

❖ Drink mineral water, diluted herbal or fruit teas, and mashed vegetables.

❖ In addition, drink apple cider vinegar and honey water three times a day.

❖ At the end of the fast, eat normally, but start slowly and carefully.

morning. Apple cider vinegar is very effective in helping all the elimination organs (intestines, lungs, skin, kidney) expel poisonous waste products from the body. You can buy a beverage with apple cider vinegar and honey on the market. It contains sweet whey and eighteen spicy herbs. Sweet whey is also perfect for cleansing the body. This special cocktail is particularly good for people with sensitive stomachs. A short detoxification fast should last about two days, during which you should take no solid food.

Effect: Cleanses the body and prevents mineral deficiencies, particularly potassium deficiencies, during a fast.

Digestive Problems

Almost 2,500 years ago, the eminent Greek physician ippocrates said, "Every malady resides in the intestines." r, reversing the idea, healthy intestines are the most nportant prerequisite for good health. Unfortunately, we ften overtax our intestines by eating too fast, too often, nd too much, particularly in the evening. The involuntary contractions of the intestines slow down, leading to harmful deposits on the walls of the intestines, which slow bowel movements, creating an unhealthy environment in the intestines.

who eat a rich

cider
helps
th when you
It cleanses the
on the tongue.

Food eaten late in the evening remains undigested during the night and starts to rot and ferment in the intestines. Stool with a strong odor is an indication that putrid bacteria are present in the intestines.

When the toxins created in the fermentation process get out of control, the body finds a sneaky way to poison itself. Toxic substances spread throughout the body in the blood stream. If this situation becomes chronic, the body's overall condition deteriorates, and the body's immune system weakens.

Toxic substances in the intestines can overtax the digestive system, causing a variety of illnesses.

Remedy for Preventing Bacterial Problems in the Intestines
Drinking a beverage of apple cider vinegar and water one to three times daily is very helpful in preventing bacterial problems in the intestines.

Additional Suggestions:
❖ Do not eat late in the evening.
❖ Eat your main meal at an earlier time.
❖ Occasionally, skip the evening meal or eat only a dry piece of toast and some tea.

Diarrhea caused by an inflammation of the small intestine, infections of the intestines, and serious food poisoning must be treated by a physician. If the diarrhea lasts more than two days or if it includes mucus or blood, fever, or stomach cramps, call your physician.

How Apple Cider Vinegar Works in the Intestines

❖ It protects against infection.

❖ It kills putrid bacteria.

❖ It helps provide a healthy intestinal environment.

❖ It helps detoxify the liver.

❖ It stimulates peristaltic action (the involuntary contractions of the intestinal walls).

If diarrhea lasts for more than two days or is severe, you should call your physician! You could be dealing with a serious infection such as dysentery, cholera, typhus, or salmonella poisoning. Apple cider vinegar can do nothing for those conditions.

Remedy for Mild Cases of Diarrhea

Applesauce made from raw, grated apples works well for diarrhea (but not for infectious enteritis). The same holds true for apple cider vinegar.

Directions: For mild diarrhea, drink (in small sips) a glass of water with 1 tsp. (5 ml) of apple cider vinegar six times a day.

Flatulence

When taken with small sips, one glass of apple cider vinegar with honey is excellent for flatulence. Those who suffer greatly should drink this beverage five minutes before eating and let each sip remain in the mouth cavity for a little while.

Effect: Increases production of saliva and, therefore, improves digestion and reduces gas-producing fermentation in the intestines.

Dizziness

If you frequently suffer from dizziness and you have no organic complications, you might want to try a treatment with apple cider vinegar.

Directions: Drink apple cider vinegar in water for four to six weeks, preferably at mealtime, but at least every morning and every night.

Effect: Balances mineral deficiencies, increases circulation, and refreshes.

Ear Noise

Drink apple cider vinegar and honey in water three times daily, ʷith your meals. This will lessen the bothersome sounds in your ... Also, drink this beverage as soon as you detect that your hearing is beginning to diminish.

Effect: Balances the minerals in your body and makes your blood flow easier.

Steam Bath for Your Ears

❖ Heat 1 cup (250 ml) of apple cider vinegar with 2 cups (500 ml) of water.

❖ Turn your head so that the steam reaches your ear, but be sure that your ear is far enough above the hot steam that it cannot hurt your ear.

Ear Pain

When your ears hurt, you must see a physician in order to determine the cause. Do not take risks with these sensitive organs!

You can treat ear pain due to inflammation or infection from a cold with a steam bath of apple cider vinegar. This will lessen the pain as well as the inflammation.

People who frequently suffer from swimmer's ear should wash their ears with a solution of two parts boiled water and one part vinegar.

Exhaustion

Now and then, we all experience periods when we feel exhausted. These usually occur after physical or mental stress. Feeling low at the end of a stressful day is perfectly normal; you simply need to take a break in order to renew yourself and regain your strength.

However, during times of exhaustion your defenses are weakened and you become more susceptible to illnesses. Drinking a beverage of apple cider every morning for a few weeks helps the body's immune system while you regain your strength or recuperate from a serious illness.

Directions: Mix 2 tsp. (10 ml) of apple cider vinegar and 1 tsp. (5 ml) of honey in a glass of water. Drink a glass first thing every morning for four to six weeks.

Effect: Strengthens the immune system, stimulates the metabolism, and fights bacteria.

You can also use apple cider vinegar as a refreshing massage. It increases blood circulation and gives you energy after strenuous

EXHAUSTION

ar
ld
nd
at
ts.
at

other risk factors, such as smoking, obesity, and lack of exercise.

Apple Cider Vinegar Massage

❖ Add 2 to 4 tbs. (30 - 60 ml) of apple cider vinegar to a glass of slightly warm water.

❖ Pour a small amount in the palm of your hand and rub your arms, shoulders, stomach, chest, and back, finish-

ing with your legs and feet.

❖ Make sure that you always massage your legs, arms, and lower body in the direction of your heart.

❖ Do not dry your skin. Let the apple cider vinegar soak into it.

physical exercise or mental stress. Diluted apple cider vinegar is an excellent natural lotion for the skin. When used over a long period of time, it tightens sagging skin.

Swollen Feet

A foot bath with apple cider vinegar has been proven to be very effective in relieving the pain of swollen and burning feet. Use the foot bath in the evening or immediately after a strenuous activity. If your feet are constantly swollen, we recommend that you bathe your feet in the morning and the evening.

Directions: Add 2 to 4 cups (.5 - 1 l) of apple cider vinegar to the water, depending on the amount of water you need to cover your feet up to your ankles. Use a container that is big enough to walk back and forth in. Do this until your feet are relaxed. When you are finished, do not dry your feet. Remove the excess water with your hand and allow the skin to dry in the air.

Effect: Stimulates the metabolism and reduces swelling.

After a foot bath in apple cider vinegar, slip into wool socks. If your legs are painful, wrap them in cloth soaked in apple cider vinegar, as recommended for "Varicose Veins," page 73.

Female Problems

You can often treat a discharge with a douche of apple cider vinegar.

Directions: Mix 3 tbs. (45 ml) of apple cider vinegar in 2 quarts (2 l) of warm water. Douche daily as long as the discharge persists. When the discharge stops, douche once a week.

Effect: Is antiseptic.

Hay Fever

Of course drinking apple cider vinegar and water every morning will not cure pollen allergies. But it can improve overall well-being and reduce bothersome symptoms, such as sneezing, watery and red eyes, skin soreness, and a general feeling of being sick.

Effect: Strengthens the immune system, balances mineral deficiencies, and stimulates the metabolism.

Headaches

In most instances, headaches are the result of nervous tension, stress, restlessness, overwork, or emotional problems. Why not try a steam bath with apple cider vinegar when such a headache comes on? Steam baths usually provide immediate relief. The steam from the apple cider vinegar invigorates and stimulates blood circulation.

Often headaches are the result of unhealthy intestinal conditions. We all experience these conditions occasionally, particularly after a rich meal late in the evening. The next morning, we feel as if our head weighs too much. Eating food too late can cause fermentation, sluggishness in the intestines, and other problems. The poison created during this process can cause a variety of complaints, not the least of which are headaches.

If the headaches are due to a late meal, drink the usual beverage of apple cider vinegar and honey over a longer period of time, perhaps twice daily, if possible on an empty stomach. This fights bacteria in the intestinal tract.

If you know that today is going to be one of those terrible headache days, rub apple cider vinegar on your forehead, temples, and neck during the day.

Heartburn

Every so often, you can relieve heartburn with a glass of apple cider vinegar and water. People who frequently suffer from a burning or scratchy sensation in their esophagus should use vinegar to flavor their food.

Heartburn is not a matter of too much stomach acid. Actually, in most cases, the cause is too little hydrochloric acid in the stomach. Hydrochloric acid and the enzyme pepsin are primarily responsible for breaking down protein. Many people who have eaten too much protein-rich food suffer from heartburn because they don't have enough hydrochloric acid.

Apple cider vinegar, together with hydrochloric acid, is helpful in softening meat, cold cuts, and similarly protein-rich foods.

However, hydrochloric acid deficiency is not always the culprit. Frequent severe heartburn may also be a sign of a stomach illness that needs medical attention and appropriate treatment.

Hemorrhoids

For itching hemorrhoids, carefully dab the affected area with undiluted apple cider vinegar every evening. In addition, drink a mixture of apple cider vinegar and water every morning.

Effect: Disinfects, increases blood clotting, and reduces swelling.

Hiccups

This is the lone exception to the rule of "no refined sugar." Take 1 tbs. (15 ml) refined sugar with five drops pure apple cider vinegar. People who do not like to eat regular sugar can use 1 tbs. (15 ml) of undiluted apple cider vinegar to balance the taste. This remedy will make hiccups disappear quickly.

Treating Hoarseness

❖ Mix 2 tbs.(30 ml) of apple cider vinegar in a glass of warm water.

❖ Take a big mouthful and gargle. Spit the water out.

❖ Take another mouthful of the mixture and drink it. This will coat areas of your throat that gargling couldn't reach.

❖ Repeat this procedure every hour. If you wake up at night, gargle again.

❖ As soon as the symptoms lessen, reduce the gargling to every two to three hours.

❖ As a preventative measure, continue to gargle after each meal for another two to three days.

Hoarseness

Often we are hoarse without quite knowing why. When we're hoarse, the vocal cords are unable to move freely, and the voice seems muffled, stressed, or even unable to produce any sound at all. Gargling with diluted apple cider vinegar is a good home remedy if the hoarseness is the result of overworked vocal cords or of a cold.

Effect: Reduces inflammation and dissolves mucus.

A throat compress using apple cider vinegar often reduces sore throat and hoarseness:

❖ Add 2 to 3 tbs. (30–45 ml) of apple cider vinegar to warm water.

❖ Soak a linen cloth in the solution, wring out the excess, and wrap the cloth around your neck. Cover the compress with a dry, warm towel. As soon as the cloth dries, repeat the process.

Hoarseness is sometimes a sign that the respiratory tract is stressed by air pollution indoors or outdoors, by smoking, or by the side effects of medication. It is important to find and eliminate the cause.

Injuries and Healing Wounds

According to an old saying, apple cider vinegar "dries" blood. The reason for the saying is that people who drink apple cider vinegar regularly find that cuts, abrasions, and wounds crust over easily and quickly. If you want a wound to heal faster, drink apple cider vinegar in water three times a day.

Effect: Disinfects and stimulates blood coagulation.

Apple cider vinegar and water is also recommended for people who suffer from frequent nosebleeds. Taking apple cider vinegar internally helps heal the arteries from the inside.

For instance, after an operation, wounds heal quicker when the patient drinks a glass of apple cider vinegar and honey in water with every meal. Experience has shown that this is particularly effective when the patient starts drinking it four weeks before the operation. Of course you may not give apple cider vinegar to a patient immediately after any operation involving the digestive system. Always consult your physician first.

Effects: Increases healing due to minerals and vitamins and supports blood coagulation.

> You may cleanse a wound with diluted vinegar water or with pure apple cider vinegar; both will disinfect and promote healing.

Insect Bites

When a bee, wasp, mosquito, or the like stings you, or if you have touched stinging nettles, immediately apply apple cider vinegar to the bite or the itching, burning area. Repeat the treatment often. It will prevent the skin from swelling too severely. However, if the rash or the bites are more serious, apple cider vinegar is only a first aid. If you are allergic to stings from jellyfish, bees, wasps, hornets, etc., seek medical attention immediately!

Effect: Reduces pain, disinfects, and reduces swelling.

Defense against Insects

Mosquitoes do not like vinegar. Rubbing apple cider vinegar in water on your skin will keep those insects away. The biting female mosquito follows its sense of smell, and it cannot resist the smell of human skin, except when that smell is covered by the smell of vinegar.

Insomnia and Chronic Exhaustion

More and more people feel tired and worn out. They use endless cups of tea, coffee, or other stimulants to help them make it through the day. By the time they leave work, they have no energy left to even think about exercising or being creative. Although they fall asleep quickly, they also wake up again, tossing and turning, unable to go back to sleep. People who suffer from chronic tiredness during the day and insomnia during the night should seriously examine their lifestyle. Often an overly stressed nervous system is the cause of the problem. This may be the result of emotional stress during times of conflict or it may be the result of overly stimulated senses. The reason could also be too many pollutants, including smoking. In addition to a reorganized lifestyle, one of the best natural remedies for insomnia and chronic exhaustion is apple cider vinegar with honey.

❖ Mix ½ cup (125 ml) of honey and 3 tbs. (45 ml) of apple cider vinegar in a glass jar.

❖ Take 2 tbs. (30 ml) of this syrup at bedtime. Under normal circumstances, you should be able to fall asleep quickly.

❖ If you are still awake in an hour, take another 2 tbs. (30 ml) of the syrup.

❖ If you wake up during the night, take 2 tbs. (30 ml) once more.

Effect: Balancing and calming because of the potassium, magnesium, and iron in apple cider vinegar. Honey is also calming.

Drinking a glass of water with 2 tsp. (10 ml) of apple cider vinegar and 2 tsp. (10ml) of honey is also very effective. Have this beverage handy in case you wake up during the night.

When you are chronically exhausted, reduce your consumption of sweets and grain products. As often as possible, eat fish and legumes spiced with apple cider vinegar. Use honey instead of sugar for sweetening. Every now and then, eat a spoonful of honey. Honey is pure energy and reaches the blood quickly. You should also consider eliminating alcohol from your diet for a while.

Intestinal Problems Caused by Spoiled Food

Maybe this has happened to you at one point or another. You are abroad, perhaps in Asia, Africa, or Latin America, and you are being very careful not to eat anything that has come in contact with the local water, since water in these regions can be contaminated with germs that cause diarrhea and stomach cramps. You're only eating fruit that can be peeled, and you've avoided fresh salad that would have been washed in local water. You've also taken the precaution of using bottled water to brush your teeth. And then it happens. On a very hot day, you order an ice-cold glass of soda, and you gulp the whole glass until only the ice cubes remain in the glass. Ice cubes? Bingo. It happened after all. You need to protect yourself immediately against a possible infection. You don't want to spoil the rest of your vacation with stomach problems and diarrhea.

Precautions against Intestinal Infections

If you consumed something that might be spoiled and could possibly infect you, drink a glass of mineral water with 2 tsp. (10 ml) of fruit vinegar.

The danger of infection is particularly great when you eat:
❖ Dishes that contain fish or shellfish

In Case of Food Poisoning

❖ Mix 1 tsp. (5 ml) of apple cider vinegar in a glass of water. Drink 1 tsp. (5 ml) at a time every five minutes.

❖ When you are finished, after three or four hours, prepare a second glass. This time, take 2 tsp. (10 ml) every five minutes.

❖ With the third glass, take a small sip every fifteen minutes.

❖ Stay in bed, drinking only diluted tea or mineral water.

Under no circumstances should you eat solid food.

❖ Eight to ten hours after the onset of the first symptoms, you should have improved enough that you can eat a dry piece of toast or a plain cracker.

❖ For two to three days after your stool returns to normal, continue to drink a glass with 1 tsp. (5 ml) of apple cider vinegar with each meal.

- ❖ Dishes containing eggs, fowl, ice, etc.
- ❖ Contaminated water
- ❖ Food that is unique to the region

If you think that a food or drink may be contaminated in some way, do without. If you can't avoid it, make sure you drink an apple cider vinegar in water before eating.

In Case of Mild Food Poisoning

If you haven't been able to take these preventive steps and have contracted mild diarrhea with stomach cramps and vomiting (possibly with other symptoms) because of spoiled food, drink apple cider vinegar and water. This destroys the harmful bacteria in the intestinal tract, detoxifies, and acts as an antibacterial agent.

Joint Pain

When joints begin to "crack," get stiff, and become painful, you may be experiencing the first signs of arthritis (inflammation of the joints). If this is the case, you should drink a cocktail made with apple cider vinegar and water every morning; better yet, drink it three times a day. Also try to eat raw vegetables and salads seasoned with apple cider vinegar.

Experience has shown that it is the acidity in the vinegar (particularly the minerals) that has such a beneficial effect on the joints. When you notice an improvement (joints move easier and are less painful), continue to drink the cocktail every morning.

Effect: Regulates calcium and sodium in the system, stimulates the metabolism, and detoxifies.

Here's a remedy that is particularly effective for joint pain. You'll need the juice of half a grapefruit, one orange, one lemon (the skins should not have been treated with chemicals), two stalks of celery, four cups (1 l) of water, apple cider vinegar, and magnesium sulfate (available at pharmacies). The

Always take a bottle of apple cider vinegar with you when you travel. If you have to eat in a questionable restaurant, be prepared. Drink apple cider vinegar with water before you eat.

Using apple cider vinegar at the first sign of food poisoning is always helpful. If the symptoms become more serious or do not improve quickly, you should seek medical care.

magnesium sulfate stimulates elimination and is highly detoxifying, one sign of which is an increase in elimination. The result is that fewer toxic substances circulate through the system, eventually reaching the joints where they can cause inflammation.

❖ Chop the celery and fruit well, including the skin. Place everything in a pot, add water, and let simmer over low heat for about an hour uncovered.

❖ As soon as the fruit is cooked, strain the liquid but rub the fruit through the sieve.

❖ Add 2 tbs.(30 ml) of apple cider vinegar and 1 tbs.(15 ml) of magnesium sulfate to the fruit.

❖ Drink one glass of the mixture with 1 tbs. (15 ml) of honey every morning.

> If you suffer from joint pain, watch your weight and make sure you get enough exercise. Swimming is the best exercise because it is gentle on the joints.

Poor Memory

When you become aware that your memory is less than it ought to be, drink a cocktail made from apple cider vinegar and honey with every meal. You will soon discover that your memory, concentration, and ability to react are improving.

D.C. Jarvis reported that in Vermont, where people drank apple cider vinegar regularly, "... it is an absolute given that men in their seventies still do a full day's work. It also is not unusual that people in their eighties still work in fields the way people much younger do." At another point he states, "Some people do their best work between the ages of sixty and eighty." And these observations were made during the 1940s and 1950s, when people seventy and eighty years old where less numerous than today. Emily Thacker, the great advocate of vinegar, insisted, "Those who drink vinegar regularly will have a clear mind all of their lives."

Effect: Refreshing and revitalizing due to the minerals and vitamins in the cocktail; improves circulation.

What You Can Do for Your Memory

❖ Drink a glass of apple cider vinegar and honey with each meal.

❖ Make sure your diet is rich in minerals and vitamins, particularly vitamin B12 (fish, milk, cheese, yeast), niacin (whole wheat, nuts, lean meat, fish, poultry, giblets, mushrooms) and folic acid (grain, green vegetables, mushrooms, legumes, whole wheat, cheese, soybeans, poultry and yeast).

❖ Try to reduce your consumption of alcohol and nicotine.

Menstruation

Drinking a glass of apple cider vinegar and honey in the morning when you have your period reduces heavy bleeding. However, because some people report that drinking apple cider vinegar on a regular basis delays the onset of their period, you should stop using it four days before the expected onset of your period.

Effect: Reduces bleeding and increases blood coagulation.

Muscle Cramps

People often wake up during the night because of cramps in their limbs, back, or neck. Drinking apple cider vinegar and water with honey for a long period of time will cause these uncomfortable cramps to disappear. It will have the same effect on muscle cramps that appear during exercise or other physical work.

Effect: Corrects mineral deficiencies.

Pulled Muscle

The old home remedy of using compresses of apple cider vinegar for pulled muscles, swellings, and bruises still works today. It reduces swelling and pain.

❖ Place a piece of cloth in pure apple cider vinegar and wring out the excess.

❖ Sprinkle a small amount of cayenne pepper on the cloth before

APPLE CIDER

Poo
m
sidei
when looking
tion. In cases of su
apple cider vinegar alone
won't be very helpful.

A Bath for Painful Muscles

❖ Add 1 to 2 cups (250 - 500 ml) of apple cider vinegar to warm bath water.

❖ Gently, massage your skin under the water, starting from your feet and working up to your neck. You might want to use a brush.

❖ After your bath, lie down and rest for a while.

To prevent injury to muscles, warm up properly before every athletic activity. Stretching exercises are particularly important.

placing it on the affected area.

❖ Cover the compress with a towel.

❖ Leave the compress in place for five to ten minutes; repeat occasionally.

Or, fold a towel several times and soak it in liquid aluminum acetate, available in health food stores and pharmacies. Remove the excess and place the towel on the affected area. Repeat when the cloth is dry.

Or, soak a towel in pure apple cider vinegar to which you have added 2 tbs. (30 ml) of iodine-containing salt. Use the towel as a compress on the affected area.

Effect: Reduces swelling and pain.

Nervous Tic

If you notice frequent and uncontrollable fluttering or twitching of your eyelids or other muscles, drink the following beverage every morning.

Mix 1 tsp. (5 ml) of apple cider vinegar in half a glass of water and add half a glass of grapefruit or orange juice. Mix well.

Effect: Corrects mineral and vitamin deficiencies.

Night Sweats

Night sweats could be an indication of a serious problem, possibly in the area of the lungs. A medical examination is necessary to determine the cause of the problem. However, you can reduce the discomfort by massaging the body with a diluted solution of apple cider vinegar before retiring.

Effect: Normalizes the pH level of the skin, cools, and calms.

If the medical examination doesn't reveal any serious organic problems, it is possible that nightly sweats are the body's attempt to rid itself of accumulated toxins. Drinking a beverage of apple cider vinegar and water every morning can speed the elimination of wastes and toxins and support the internal cleansing process of the body.

Nosebleed

If you suffer from frequent nosebleeds, drink apple cider vinegar regularly. You can stop the bleeding by soaking a small piece of cotton in vinegar and gently inserting it into the nostril. Leave it in place until the bleeding stops.

Effect: Increases coagulation and disinfects.

Pain

The following gentle pain remedy from nature's apothecary is helpful in relieving minor pain.

In case of headaches, nerve pain, muscle pain, or any other type of pain, place a few drops of the Pain-Relief Tincture (see box on the next page) on a piece of cotton and rub the painful area. This is particularly effective at bedtime.

The tincture is also effective for acne.

Effect: Reduces pain and is calming.

Pay attention to chronic pain. It may be a sign of organic problems that must be treated by a physician. The same is true of severe pain that appears suddenly.

Pain-Relief Tincture

❖ Grate 1 lb. (500 g) of horseradish and place in a glass jar with 2 cups (500 ml) of apple cider vinegar.

❖ Close the lid tightly and store for two to three weeks in a cool, dark place.

❖ Separate the liquid.

Complaints during Pregnancy

You can easily lessen morning sickness by eating an apple. Try to drink a glass of apple cider vinegar and honey in water. If you can't handle this on a empty stomach, drink the cocktail after breakfast. By the way, women who drink this powerful cocktail throughout their pregnancy are supposed to have babies with strong constitutions and healthy, thick hair and strong fingernails. Supposedly, these babies also have fewer problems with teething.

Effect: Provides minerals, stimulates the metabolism, and strengthens the placenta.

> You can lessen morning sickness and nausea during pregnancy by soaking a towel in warm apple cider vinegar and placing it on your stomach. When the cloth cools off, repeat the procedure.

Rheumatism and Gout

Drinking a beverage with fruit vinegar first thing in the morning helps prevent rheumatism and gout.

Effect: Detoxifies and protects the intestines from poisonous substances that could enter the body.

Skin Rashes

Applying diluted apple cider vinegar on skin rashes reduces the itching and burning. If you can tolerate it, you may want to experiment with a stronger solution or even use pure apple cider vinegar. You can also make a paste using apple cider vinegar and corn starch. Apply the paste to the affected areas. When the paste dries, the skin should not itch anymore. If larger areas of the skin are affected, you can add 2 to 3 cups (500 - 750 ml) of apple cider vinegar to your bath water. If you like the fragrance, you may also add essential oil of thyme. In addition, drink apple cider vinegar in water at every meal. (At the very least, drink it in the morning.) If the skin rash turns out to be contact eczema or the result of an allergy, drink apple cider vinegar and water with every meal until the rash is gone.

Effect: Supplies minerals, particularly potassium; and reduces inflammation.

Also, if your skin is prickly, as if hundreds of ants are crawling over it, rub the affected area with a solution of apple cider vinegar (mix 1:1).

Sunburn

Gently apply diluted apple cider vinegar to painful, sunburned skin. You may also soak a soft cloth in apple cider vinegar and place it on the affected skin. Add 2 cups (500 ml) of apple cider vinegar to lukewarm water for a very cooling bath.

Effect: Cools and calms the skin and disinfects.

Sore Throat

Germs cause sore throats. Since apple cider vinegar has antibacterial and anti-inflammatory properties, it is a gentle remedy for a sore throat due to a cold.

Directions: Mix ¼ cup (62.5 ml) of honey with ¼ cup (62.5 ml) of apple cider vinegar. Take 1 tsp. (5 ml) of this mixture every three to four hours. Stir the mixture thoroughly every time.

Alternate directions: Mix ¼ cup (62.5 ml) of water, ¼ cup (62.5 ml) of apple cider vinegar, 2 tsp. (10 ml) of honey, and ½ tsp. (2.5 ml) of cayenne pepper. Mix well. Take 1 tsp.(5 ml) every two to three hours. If needed, you may take it more often.

Effect: Kills bacteria, dissolves mucus, and reduces inflammation. Gargling with apple cider vinegar also reduces the pain of a sore throat (see "Hoarseness").

Sometimes skin rashes are the result of a mineral deficiency. For that reason, apple cider vinegar is often an ideal remedy. Also, use sea salt in your kitchen. It is rich in minerals!

If your throat continues to be sore for several days, you may have a serious illness caused by streptococcus bacteria. These infections need to be treated by a physician!

A Hot Drink for a Throat Infection

❖ Add 1 tbs. (15 ml) of honey and 1 to 2 tbs. (15 - 30 ml) of apple cider vinegar.

❖ Drink the mixture several times a day, using small sips.

Tired Eyes

Soak two cotton pads in apple cider vinegar. Close your eyes and place the pads on your eyelids. They will refresh tired eyes. Leave the pads on for a time. After you remove them, wash the area with lukewarm water.

Drinking apple cider vinegar and water with 2 tsp. (10 ml) of honey every morning helps eyes that tire quickly when reading or watching television. It also helps eyes that react to bright lights. The beta-carotene in apple cider vinegar also prevents cataracts.

Effect: Strengthens eyesight because of the minerals in the apple cider vinegar.

Tooth and Gum Diseases

People who suffer from cavities or inflamed gums should drink apple cider vinegar in water regularly with each meal. Rinsing the mouth with apple cider vinegar in water (but without honey) prevents tartar buildup, reduces inflammation, and removes the breeding ground for germs.

Effect: Fights bacteria, reduces inflammation, and provides minerals, particularly calcium.

According to a study, eating apples regularly can also help prevent cavities. Chewing an apple cleanses the space between the teeth, and the acidity in apples prevents the development of plaque, a film of bacteria.

Increased Levels of Triglycerides in the Blood

Elevated levels of triglycerides in the blood are usually the result of too many animal fats (meat, eggs, and milk products) in the diet. Over time, increased levels thicken the blood and can lead

Apple-Cider-Vinegar Water for Dental Hygiene

❖ Add 1 tsp. (5 ml) of apple cider vinegar to a glass of water and mix well.

❖ Rinse your mouth with this solution and gargle vig-

orously in the morning and the evening after brushing your teeth.

❖ Over time, your teeth will be whiter.

to metabolic illnesses, reduce the flow of blood, cause harden
ing of the arteries, and, worst case scenario, entirely close art′
ies, leading to heart attacks and strokes .Drinking a beve
with apple cider vinegar is helpful in thinning the blood,
ing it to flow easier. By the way, eating fruits, such aʳ
grapes, and cranberries, and drinking the juices of these ⸍
can produce the same effects.

Directions: Use 2 tsp. (10 ml) of apple cider vinegar to a glass
of water every morning over a long period of time.

Effect: Apple pectin lowers dangerous LDL cholesterol, easing
blood flow.

Varicose Veins

Rubbing painful varicose veins in the morning and in the
evening with undiluted apple cider vinegar has proven to be
quite effective.

Place a piece of cloth in undiluted apple cider vinegar, wring
out the excess, and wrap the cloth around the legs. Cover the

*When your legs are tired,
heavy, swollen, or painful in
the evening, elevate them and
rub them with apple cider
vinegar.*

Steam Bath of Apple Cider Vinegar

❖ Mix equal parts of apple cider vinegar and water in a small container.

❖ Heat the mixture on the stove.

❖ As soon as steam develops, hold your head over the container and cover your head with a large towel, preventing the steam from escaping.

❖ Breathe deeply through your nose. Close your eyes and allow the steam to envelop your head.

❖ Inhale the steam for as long as it is comfortable, but for no more than five minutes.

❖ If possible, rest quietly afterwards.

cloth with a towel. Elevate the legs and leave the wrap on for thirty minutes. Use these wraps twice an day, morning and evening, for at least six weeks, and the pain should disappear. In addition, drink a glass of apple cider vinegar and honey every morning. You also need to have sufficient exercise (walking, running, biking, etc.).

Effect: Promotes healing of unduly enlarged blood vessels in much the same way that it aids in coagulating the blood in injuries.

However, if the varicose veins are severe, apple cider vinegar will only reduce the pain. If varicose veins worsen, you should see your physician.

Apple cider vinegar and honey in water is helpful for people who are sensitive to changes in the weather and for people who suffer from nervous tension or exhaustion when the weather is particularly hot. These are conditions that are often troublesome for older people.

Warts

The following mixture is helpful for treating warts, horny projections on the skin.

❖ Mix 1 tsp. (5 ml) of salt and 4 tsp. (20 ml) of apple cider vinegar in a small glass jar. Close the jar and shake well.

❖ Dab the warts with this tincture several times a day for a long period of time.

Sensitivity to Changes in the Weather

Experience has shown that drinking a beverage of apple cider vinegar and honey in water twice a day lessens the negative effects of weather changes, such as headaches, tiredness, irritability, joint pains, and poor performance.

Weight Problems

People who do not deal with the reasons for their weight gain and who continue to overeat, use too much salt, sugar, and fat, and who don't exercise won't be able to lose weight even with the help of apple cider vinegar. But for people who are already practicing moderation, are committed to a well-balanced diet and prudent exercise in fresh air, apple cider vinegar will make losing easier and faster. Apple cider vinegar stimulates the metabolism, helps break down fats, detoxifies, supports digestion, helps remove excess water, and curbs the appetite. It also reduces the desire for sweets. Dr. D. C. Jarvis told us, "Those who have a glass of water with a teaspoon (5 ml) of fruit vinegar will eat less because they feel satisfied much faster."

Trying to lose weight requires considerable self-discipline over a long period of time. But even willpower won't guarantee permanent success until you change the lifestyle that was responsible for the extra weight.

Beverage When Overweight

❖ While you are losing weight, drink a glass of water with 2 tsp (10 ml) of vinegar with each meal.

❖ When you reach your ideal weight, continue to drink a glass of apple cider vinegar and water in the morning. This supports digestion and adds to your well-being.

Apple Cider Vinegar for Hygiene

Apple cider vinegar is a tried and tested remedy for beautiful skin and hair.

Apple cider vinegar is a natural skin product that stimulates skin function, increases circulation, tightens and smoothes skin, and is refreshing and invigorating. It is surprisingly versatile, and its healing effects are useful for a variety of purposes.

Acid Mantle as Protection

The essence of skin care is mild cleansing that does not destroy the acid mantle of the skin.

The acid mantle of the skin, the result of the evaporation of sour perspiration, slows down the development of many germs that cause illness. The surface of the skin, which is slightly acidic and dry, performs a very important protective function for the whole body. However, most soaps strip this acid mantle from the skin because they are highly alkaline. Itching skin or scalp is usually a sign that the cleansing medium was too strong, disturbing the natural acid condition of the skin. Dr. D. C. Jarvis said, "If we use something sour to clean our body, we give the skin what is normally beneficial: acidity." He suggests that instead of soap we should take a bath with fruit vinegar in the water or at least rub the skin with a solution of fruit vinegar and water after we have used soap so that "the skin maintains its normal acidic reaction." The skin will be rosy and have a sufficient supply of blood , a sign of vibrant skin. Vinegar has almost the same pH value as healthy skin (5.5). Rubbing your skin with fruit vinegar renews its protective mantle and is highly recommended as a natural skin lotion.

Daily Skin Care

Massage with Apple Cider Vinegar

Mix 2 tbs. (30 ml) of apple cider vinegar in 1 quart (1 l) of water and use this solution on your whole body. Proceed as recommended in "Exhaustion," page 57 (massage with apple cider vinegar). In addition, rubbing your body with apple-cider-vinegar water removes soap residues and, for a short time, acts as a deodorant. People who do not have the time for a total massage every day should have it at least once every week.

Full Bath

For a full bath, add about 1 cup (250 ml) of apple cider vinegar to the bath water. Remain in the water for at least fifteen minutes so that the skin is able to absorb the acidity. A vinegar bath regenerates tired and feeble skin.

Apple Cider Vinegar and Lavender

You can create a particularly good lotion by mixing apple cider vinegar with lavender blossoms. This additive soothes and clears up bad skin.
❖ Place a handful of lavender blossoms in a glass jar and add a 1 cup (250 ml) of apple cider vinegar.
❖ Close the jar tightly and place it in a cool and dark place for two to three weeks.
❖ Separate the liquid and use it in bath water.

Apple Cider Vinegar: A Natural Deodorant

To prevent body odor, apply apple cider vinegar on a washcloth to your underarm area after you shower. This is effective and gentle for your skin. It inhibits the growth of the bacteria that cause body odor, but it doesn't interfere with the natural protective condition of the skin.

During the so-called dog days of summer, a foot bath with 1 or 2 cups (250–500 ml) of apple cider vinegar in cool water is a very refreshing experience.

Caring for Your Face

Oily skin

You can use apple cider, a gently disinfecting substance, in many different formulas and combine it with additional ingredients.

A Mask of Strawberries and Apple Cider Vinegar

A mask made of strawberries and apple cider vinegar clears, calms, and removes oils from the skin. It refreshes, protects, and disinfects.

❖ Mash five strawberries with a fork and add 3 tbs. (45 ml) of apple cider vinegar.

❖ Allow the mixture to rest for two to three hours; separate the liquid and apply to your face.

❖ Allow the mask to remain on your face overnight.

❖ Rinse your face in the morning and apply moisturizing cream.

Face Lotion

In cases of oily skin, mix equal parts of mineral water and apple cider vinegar. Use the lotion in the morning and evening to cleanse your face.

Rose Vinegar Lotion

Mix 5 tbs. (75 ml) of apple cider vinegar with 5 tbs. (75 ml) of mineral water. Place a handful of dried rose petals in a glass jar and cover them with apple cider vinegar and the mineral water. Close the jar and allow the mixture to rest for two to three weeks in a cool, dark place. Separate the liquid. Do not wash after you have applied the lotion.

This lotion is for those with oily skin and those who tend to have bad skin. You may also use the lotion as an additive for a very soothing bath.

Facial Peeling

A facial peeling removes the dead surface layer from the skin. It works for every type of skin.

❖ Cleanse your face with a mild cleansing lotion.

❖ Use warm water and a small terry-cloth towel. Press the towel against your skin for one to two minutes.

❖ Add 2 or 3 tbs. (30–45 ml) of apple cider vinegar to lukewarm water and soak a linen cloth in the water.

Place this cloth on your face and cover it with a damp, comfortably warm towel.

❖ Wait five minutes, rinse your face with warm water, and vigorously rub with a damp towel. This will remove the surface layer that was softened. Underneath, you will discover fresh, rosy skin.

❖ This is a gentle procedure that you should use once a week in the evening.

Dry and Mature Skin

For dry skin, we have two recipes in which you add a fatty substance to the apple cider vinegar.

A Mask of Avocados and Vinegar

Ingredients: Two egg yolks, 2 tbs. (30 ml) of apple cider vinegar, 2 tsp. (10 ml) of thistle oil, 2 tsp. (10 ml) of fresh avocado, and 1 tsp. (5 ml) of lemon juice.

❖ Beat the egg yolks in a mixer until foamy; add the apple cider vinegar and the thistle oil, one drop at a time.

❖ Mash the avocado with a fork and mix with lemon juice.

❖ Add the avocado mixture to the foam. Use immediately.

This mask is very gentle on dry and mature skin. Apply it in the evening after you have cleaned your skin and leave it on

You'll have to experiment with these cosmetic preparations and observe the results carefully because everyone's skin reacts differently. Give yourself enough time to find out what works for you.

overnight. In the morning, rinse your face with clear water. Store any leftover mixture in the refrigerator and use it the next evening.

A Mask of Wheat Germ and Vinegar

❖ Gently warm 4 tbs. (60 ml) of apple cider vinegar (do not allow to boil).
❖ Add 3 tsp. (15 ml) of honey and 2 tsp. (10 ml) of wheat germ.
❖ Add the mask to your clean face and allow it to remain for half an hour. Remove with lukewarm water.

Wheat germ is available in health food stores and regular grocery stores.

The fats and oils, as well as the vitamins and minerals, contained in avocados make them an ideal soothing substance for internal and external application.

Oral Hygiene ✓

Bad Breath

To fight the bad taste you sometimes wake with, or bad breath in general, gargle with a mixture of 1 tsp. (5 ml) of apple cider vinegar in a glass of water.

Discolored Teeth ✓

In case of discolored teeth, brush your teeth with 1 tsp. (5 ml) of apple cider vinegar and water, and afterwards, rinse your mouth for a minute with the same solution.

Caring for Your Hair

Hair Loss ✓

It is perfectly normal to lose about 100 strands of hair every morning. During pregnancy and in the fall or spring, you can lose even more. If you notice that you lose more hair than usual or if you discover bald spots, the reason might be a disturbance in your metabolism. We recommend that you drink a glass of apple cider vinegar and water with each meal for at least six to eight weeks. This will regulate your metabolism, correct mineral deficiencies, and stabilize hair growth.

You can also massage your scalp with diluted apple cider vinegar. Unless hair loss is hereditary or is due to a particular illness, it will quickly start to grow again.

Hair Rinse ✓

Rinsing your hair with 3 cups (750 ml) of warm water to which you've added ¼ cup (62.5 ml) of apple cider vinegar will make your hair soft, shiny, and easy to comb. It will also intensify your hair color. To get the best results, use this rinse after every shampoo.

An Organic Rinse for Hair and Scalp

❖ Steep dry stinging nettle, available at health food stores, in warm apple cider vinegar; separate the liquid.

❖ Gently massage into your hair and scalp, one section at a time.

❖ Do not rinse again.

❖ Let the smell evaporate (this won't take long).

You may also add 1 tsp. (5 ml) of birch leaves and 1 tsp. (5 ml) of lavender blossoms to the hair rinse. This is beneficial for all types of hair.

Herbal Rinse

The ingredients for a herbal rinse are a few teaspoons of dried flowers or herbs, 3 oz. (100 ml) of water and 1½ oz. (60 ml) of apple cider vinegar.

Depending on your hair type, add additional ingredients:
❖ For oily hair, add 1 tsp. (5 ml) of sage, rosemary, and thyme.
❖ For tired, limp hair, add 1 tsp. (5 ml) each of stinging nettle leaves, rosemary, and chamomile flowers.
❖ For dull hair, add two tbs. (30 ml) of dried and chopped burdock root.

Pour boiling water over the herbs or blossoms; allow the mixture to steep for fifteen minutes; separate the liquid.
❖ Mix this solution with apple cider vinegar.
❖ Use this herbal potion to rinse your hair after shampooing.
❖ Do not rinse out; towel-dry hair.

Here is a recipe for itching scalp: Add 1 tsp. (5 ml) of apple cider vinegar to a glass of water. Dip your comb in the solution and comb through your hair, one strand at a time, until you have thoroughly saturated your hair and scalp. Allow your hair to dry naturally; do not use a hair dryer.

Dandruff

Dandruff on your scalp is perfectly normal because the body sheds dead skin cells continuously. However, you can treat severe dandruff with apple cider vinegar. Apply diluted apple cider vinegar directly to the scalp after shampooing. This is also a remedy for itching scalp.

❖ Pour a little apple cider vinegar in a small glass jar
❖ Dip a damp washcloth in apple cider vinegar and rub the scalp, section by section.
❖ Leave on for at least for thirty minutes.
❖ Shampoo hair as usual.
❖ In case of severe dandruff, treat the scalp every time you shampoo your hair.

Setting Lotion with Honey

Ingredients: One tbs. (15 ml) of honey, 1 cup (250 ml) of distilled water, 1 tsp. (5 ml) of apple cider vinegar.

❖ Warm the water, but don't let it come to a boil; dissolve the honey and add the vinegar.
❖ Towel-dry your hair and apply the lotion before you use the blow dryer.
❖ If you want to lighten the color of your hair, use chamomile flowers instead of water; then add vinegar and honey.
❖ To add a reddish tint to your hair, dissolve 1 tbs. (15 ml) of red henna to the distilled water, let simmer for ten minutes, and add honey and vinegar.

Caring for Your Hands

Chapped Hands ✓

If you mix olive oil and apple cider vinegar in equal parts, you'll have a skin oil that will heal your chapped hands. Use this mixture every time you wash your hands and before you go to bed. (Wear a pair of cotton gloves to protect the sheets.) Your hands will be smooth and soft in no time. This mixture also works well on the rest of your body.

Rub apple cider vinegar into your fingernails before you apply nail polish. Your nails will be free of oil, and the polish will last longer.

Splitting and Breaking Fingernails

As is the case with hair loss, discolored and brittle fingernails indicate deficiencies of silicic acid, calcium, and sodium. Since these are plentiful in apple cider vinegar, drinking it regularly over a longer period of time will correct the condition. However, you must drink the apple cider vinegar for at least six weeks.

Vinegar is not in competition with modern disinfecting substances that kill germs with chemical thoroughness. Vinegar is much gentler, and sometimes that is an advantage.

Age Spots

You can lighten age spots with a mixture of apple cider vinegar and onion juice.

❖ Mix 1 tsp. (5 ml) of onion juice with 2 tsp. (10 ml) of apple cider vinegar.

❖ Apply the liquid in the evening and leave on overnight. Do not wash your hands until the next morning.

❖ Apply this juice regularly, and, in time, the brown spots will fade.

Caring for Your Feet

Hard Skin and Calluses

A foot bath made with apple cider vinegar effectively fights perspiration and foot odor. Mix two parts of water with two parts of apple cider vinegar.

Treat hard patches, calluses, or corns with compresses of apple cider vinegar.

❖ Bathe your feet in warm soapy water for ten minutes. Dry well.

❖ Saturate a piece of gauze in pure apple cider vinegar and apply to the affected area.

❖ Secure the gauze with a bandage or wear cotton socks.

❖ Leave on overnight. Repeat several times until the hard skin and calluses are gone.

Apple Cider Vinegar in the Kitchen

Sweet and sour delicacies: fruits and vegetables.

I f you do not like the taste of apple cider vinegar but want to take advantage of its healthy benefits, think about how you can use it in your kitchen. If you use apple cider vinegar for cooking and salad dressings, you can provide your family with all the positive substances found in apple cider vinegar. You may use apple cider vinegar in all recipes that call for vinegar. In American and English kitchens, we use this vinegar almost exclusively for cooking and seasoning. By the way, statistics tell us that almost sixty percent of all the vinegar sold is used for salad dressings. Many products, such as mustard, ketchup, mayonnaise, chutney, and seltzer contain vinegar.

Tricks in the Kitchen with Apple Cider Vinegar

You can use apple cider vinegar in a variety of gentle and natural ways in the kitchen.

Tenderizing

Legumes and cabbage dishes become softer and easier to digest if you add a bit of apple cider vinegar while they are cooking. In addition, apple cider vinegar brings out the flavor of the food. If you keep poultry or veal in the refrigerator for a day or two, wrap the meat in a cloth soaked in diluted apple cider vinegar (1:1). The meat will remain fresher longer and be more tender.

To tenderize a roast, take equal parts of stock and apple cider vinegar and bring to a boil. Allow to cool and place the roast in this mixture for a few hours. Then, proceed as you normally would. For steaks, make a marinade from vinegar, oil, and, if you

Pay special attention to quality when shopping for naturally cloudy apple cider vinegar for cooking purposes. This is produced from whole, completely ripe apples and is only available in health food stores. Few supermarkets offer natural apple cider vinegar.

like, crushed garlic. Stir well and pour the marinade over the steaks. Let rest for two hours, turning the steaks occasionally.

Pickling Solution for Meat Dishes

You can use a pickling solution for game, turkey, wild boar, beef, and lamb. One way to do this is to allow the meat to remain in the solution over a long period of time. The other way is to allow it to sit for only twenty-four hours.

Ingredients for pickling solution: Three cups (750 ml) of water, 1 cup (250 ml) of apple cider vinegar, herbs and vegetables normally used to make soup, one or two onions cut in rings, a piece of lemon peel (organic), 1 to 2 tsp. (5–10 ml) of juniper berries, four to five mustard seeds, four to five pepper corns, three to four cloves, two to three bay leaves, and, depending on your taste, sage, thyme, and rosemary. Don't add salt to this pickling solution; you only add salt to the meat after you remove it from the solution.

If you decide to use the former method, mix all the ingredients, boil, and let the mixture cool. Boiling the pickling solution makes it spicier and adds to its preserving ability. You pour the cold solution over the meat, covering it completely. If you don't have enough of the mixture, you must turn the meat daily. You can leave the meat in the solution anywhere from two to seven days. How long depends on the age of the animal and the thickness of the meat. Cover the meat and keep it in a cool place. The "quick method" is similar. You boil the ingredients and pour the pickling solution over the meat while the solution is still hot. Store the meat in a cold place. You can cook the meat after twenty-four hours. The meat retains much of the natural substances that leech out if it sits in the marinade for a longer period of time.

Preventing Oxidation

To prevent fruit and vegetables from turning brown, pour diluted apple cider vinegar over them. Peeled raw potatoes won't turn brown if you keep them in a jar with apple-cider-vinegar water, but you should use them the next day.

> A pickling solution made with apple cider vinegar makes meat more digestible and tender, and enhances the flavor of some meats, while lessening the flavor of others, game and lamb, for instance.

Deodorizer

Adding vinegar to fish dishes or fish soups removes the unpleasant fish odor. Pouring vinegar over the fish also works well. When steamed, the fish will retain its white color.

Keeping Food

Fresh meat or fresh fish will keep longer in a vinegar marinade that you store in a cool place. Marinade acts as a preservative, adds a tart flavor, tenderizes tough meat, and reduces the strong flavor of game. Cheese also will keep longer and will not dry out as quickly if you wrap it in a cloth soaked in vinegar and place it in the refrigerator.

Neutralizing

If you have used too much salt, mix apple cider vinegar and sugar in equal parts and add the mixture, a teaspoon (5 ml) at a time, until the salty taste is gone. If the mixture is too sweet, add apple cider vinegar until the sweetness is gone.

Asparagus remains fresh when wrapped in a kitchen towel soaked in apple cider vinegar. You can keep it in the refrigerator for a couple of hours or even for a day.

Treating meat with a marinade or pickling solution keeps it fresh longer, makes it digestible, and tenderizes it. In addition, a marinade or pickling solution gives meat a very delicate sour flavor.

Kitchen Tips

❖ If you add a dash of apple cider vinegar to the water when you boil eggs, the egg whites won't escape into the water if one of the eggshells break.

❖ Adding 1 tsp. (5 ml) of apple cider vinegar to jelly will make it remain solid, even when the temperature is very high.

❖ Add 2 tbs. (30 ml) of apple cider vinegar and a dash of salt to the water that you use to rinse lettuce, vegetables, and fruit. This removes residues of pesticides and soil.

❖ Add 1 tsp. (5 ml) of apple cider vinegar to the fat you use for deep frying. The food won't absorb as much fat and will be more digestible.

Classic Recipe for Salad Dressing and Marinades

Apple cider vinegar is a good and inexpensive vinegar that works well in all salad dressings. The best, most delicious, and healthiest salad dressing (which you can also use for green vegetables) is made with 2 tbs. (30 ml) of olive oil, 1 tbs. (15 ml) of apple cider vinegar, a dash of honey, mustard, fresh herbs, a dash of horseradish, and freshly ground pepper.

All-Vegetable Appetizer

Here is a vitamin-rich appetizer to start a sophisticated meal in style. Arrange sliced tomatoes, cucumbers, olives, onion rings, one egg cut into quarters, and Greek goat cheese on a plate. Add salad dressing.

Fragrant Herb Mixture for Salad

Using 1 tbs. (15 ml) of the following herb mixture will give a salad a wonderful, delicate aroma. Since this mixture will keep in the refrigerator, it is always available.

Chop as many different ingredients as you like. For instance, you might want to use parsley, chives, watercress, chervil, borage, dill, sorrel, etc. Place this in a glass jar and add 2 tbs. (30 ml) of oil and 2 tsp. (10 ml) of apple cider vinegar. Close the jar tightly and store it in the refrigerator.

> Since mayonnaise consists primarily of vegetable oil, it is high in fat. Adding vinegar enhances its flavor and makes it more digestible.

Homemade Mayonnaise

❖ Place an egg, 1 tbs. (15 ml) of apple cider vinegar, 1 cup (250 ml) of oil, 1 tsp. (5 ml) of mustard, salt, and a dash of sugar one at a time into a bowl.

❖ Everything should be at room temperature in order to make a smooth mixture and to obtain the best results.

❖ Insert the hand-held mixer into the ingredients, then turn it on. Slowly lift and lower the mixer until the mayonnaise is finished.

Vinegar Recipes

You can create delicately balanced, flavorful dishes when using apple cider vinegar for the following recipes.

Garlic Vinegar

Vinegar with a slight garlic aroma enhances the flavor of all salad greens. However, don't add fresh garlic to your salad.

Ingredients: Fifteen to twenty garlic cloves, a small parsley root, 1 tsp.(5 ml) of pepper corns, three bay leaves, 1 tsp. (5 ml) each of thyme, oregano, basil , and 1 quart (1 l) of apple cider vinegar.

Preparation: Place the vinegar, garlic cloves (peeled and cut in half), parsley root, and spices in a pot. Bring to a boil and allow to simmer for five minutes. Separate the liquid and pour into a bottle. Return the pepper corns and pieces of garlic to the liquid. Store the bottle for four weeks in a cool dark place until the vinegar has matured.

Raspberry Vinegar

Ingredients: Two lb. (1 kg) of raspberries, 3 cups (750 ml) of apple cider vinegar, and a small vanilla pod.

Preparation: Check, rinse, and crush raspberries with a fork. Add 1 cup (250 ml) of apple cider vinegar and the vanilla pod and allow the whole mixture to rest for six days. Stir the mixture once a day. Separate the liquid, add the remaining apple cider vinegar, pour the liquid into a bottle, and seal the bottle.

Lemon and Orange Vinegar

Ingredients: Half an orange, the peel from an organic orange and a lemon, 2 tsp. (10 ml) of lemon balm leaves, 1 quart (1 l) of apple cider vinegar.

Preparation: Peel the orange and cut it into small pieces. Cut the orange peel and the lemon peel into small oblong strips. Place the orange meat, the peel from the lemon and the orange, and the lemon balm leaves in a bottle. Add the apple cider vinegar. Seal the bottle and allow to rest in a cool dark place for three weeks.

Always add a dab of apple cider vinegar to meat dishes, sauces, and stews. This enhances the flavor and adds all the positive substances contained in apple cider vinegar.

Apple cider vinegar lessens the sense of hunger. People who sometimes have to skip a meal, or would like to skip a meal, will find that their hunger pains diminish after they drink a glass of apple cider vinegar and honey in water.

If you want to bring the aroma of fresh herbs into your kitchen in the winter, store them in apple cider vinegar. The vinegar will take on the fragrance of the herbs. Adding this vinegar to your food will give your dishes the delicate fragrance of the herbs.

Honey Vinegar

Ingredients: Four tbs. (60 ml) of honey, two small shot glasses of Grand Marnier, the juice of a lemon and an orange, 3 cups (750 ml) of apple cider vinegar.

Preparation: Mix all ingredients in a pot and allow the mixture to come to a quick boil. Pour the liquid into a bottle, close tightly, and allow to rest for two to three weeks in a cool and dark place.

Sage Vinegar

Ingredients: Two twigs of sage, half a lemon (organic), and 2 cups (500 ml) of apple cider vinegar.

Preparation: Allow the sage to dry for two days; cut the lemon in large chunks. Add all the ingredients to a glass jar, close tightly, and let rest for two weeks in a cool and dark place. Pour the vinegar into a decorative bottle and seal airtight.

A Gift Idea with Tarragon

A beautiful bottle filled with homemade tarragon vinegar is a welcome gift. Your hostess will appreciate your gesture and will enjoy using your gift.

Tarragon vinegar adds a delicate flavor to all light sauces, particularly to béarnaise sauce, mushroom dishes, and veal or poultry ragout.

Ingredients: One quart (1 l) apple cider vinegar, a handful of freshly picked tarragon leaves, two shallots, two bay leaves, and a few peppers.

Preparation: Rinse the tarragon leaves and place them in a large glass jar. You may also add shallots, bay leaves, and pepper. Pour boiling vinegar over the ingredients and tightly close the glass jar. Allow to rest for two to three weeks in a cool dark place. Then, pour the contents through a cheese cloth. Sterilize a nicely shaped bottle by boiling it. Pour the vinegar into the bottle. Add a twig of fresh tarragon to the vinegar. Be sure the tarragon twig is totally immersed in the vinegar so that it doesn't become moldy. Boil a new cork for a few minutes to kill all the germs. Use the cork to seal the bottle.

Colorful, crunchy, ⌐
mer salads taste particu⌐
good when you use two or thre⌐
different kinds of vinegar to
make the dressing. You can do
the same with olive oil. Try
mixing olive oil and walnut oil.

Delicious Sauces

Vinaigrette

In French, vinegar is *vinaigre*, which means wine (*vin*) that has turned sour (*aigre*). This is the root of the word "vinaigrette," a salad dressing flavored with vinegar.

Ingredients: Two hard-boiled eggs, 3 tbs. (45 ml) of thistle oil, 2 tbs. (30 ml) of apple cider vinegar, freshly ground white pepper, a dash of sea salt, a few capers, and 1 tsp. (5 ml) of hot mustard.

Preparation: Finely crush the hard-boiled eggs with a fork. Stir them into a sauce with the other ingredients, except for the capers, which you add at the end. Instead of capers, you may also use finely cubed spring onions, a crushed garlic clove, and finely chopped herbs (dill, basil).

Vinaigrette is excellent with tomatoes, all leafy salads, beans, potatoes, and artichokes.

91

...s sauce
...ral Italy.
Rou... ...d, "salsa"
means "g.... ... sauce." It goes particularly well with hard-boiled eggs and cold beef.

Salsa Verde

Ingredients: a bunch of parsley, three fillets of sardines (bones removed), a pickle, a boiled potato, a garlic clove, a shallot, 1 tbs. (15 ml) of olive oil, and 1 tbs. (15 ml) of apple cider vinegar.

Preparation: Finely chop the parsley. Cut the sardines into strips. Push the boiled potato through a sieve and cube the garlic clove and shallots. Stir all together with the olive oil and vinegar.

Hot Steak Sauce

This sauce goes well with grilled meat or steak and is also an excellent sauce for fondue. If you like your food less spicy, simply reduce the amount of pepperoni and Tabasco sauce and replace them with a little bit of pepper. Of course, you may also leave out the whiskey.

Ingredients: One cup (250 ml) of tomato ketchup, 1 tbs. (15 ml) of buckthorn, a dash of whiskey, two to three small slices of pepperoni, a dash of pepper, a dash of Tabasco sauce, 4 tbs. (60 ml) of apple cider vinegar.

Preparation: Cut the pepperoni in small pieces and mix all the ingredients together well. Presto! The "devil's sauce" is ready.

Depending on your taste, you may also enhance this sauce with crushed garlic or a small crushed onion, freshly ground horseradish, or a small amount of a grated apple and Worcestershire sauce.

Curry Cream for Light Fish Dishes

This delicately flavored curry sauce is ideal for chicken, turkey, and fish.

Ingredients: An onion, 1½ tbs. (20 g) of butter, 1 tbs. (15 ml) of flour (you may substitute corn starch or arrow root), ½ cup (125 ml) of instant chicken broth, 2 tbs. (30 ml) of apple cider vinegar, 2 tbs. (30 ml) of curry, and ½ cup (125 ml) of sweet cream.

Preparation: Melt the butter and saute the finely chopped onion. Add the flour and then the chicken broth in small amounts. Allow the mixture to simmer over a low flame for five minutes. Add the curry and apple cider vinegar and stir well. At the very end, add the sweet cream; the sauce should not boil again.

Asparagus Sauce

Serve this sauce with asparagus and other vegetables, such as cauliflower. It also is very good with cold meat.

Ingredients: Two hard-boiled eggs, 1 tbs. (15 ml) of extra-virgin olive oil, a dash of salt and pepper, 1 tbs. (15 ml) of apple cider vinegar, a pickle, two shallots, 2 tbs. (30 ml) of capers, a small amount of garlic, and fresh garden herbs, including chives.

Preparation: Crush the boiled egg yolk with a fork and mix with the vinegar, oil, salt, and pepper. Finely chop the egg white, pickles, shallots, and capers. If you like, add crushed garlic. Add the finely chopped herbs at the end.

Indian Apple Chutney

Chutney comes from India. It is a highly spiced sauce preserved with vinegar and sugar.

Apple chutney stimulates the appetite. It is a fruity addition to grilled meat, veal cutlets, pork, and poultry dishes.

Ingredients: Two lb. (1 kg) of apple (not too sweet), two to three large onions, 3½ oz. (100 g) of shelled walnuts, ½ cup (125 ml) of apple cider vinegar, 7 oz. (250 g) of dark candy, the juice from half a lemon, two to three fresh leaves of sage, ½ tsp. (2.5 ml) of mustard powder, a pinch each of cinnamon, ginger powder, and pimento, and, according to taste, 1 to 2 tsp. (5 - 10 ml) of chili sauce.

Preparation: Wash the apples, remove the seeds, and chop into small pieces. Cube the onions and break the walnuts in half. Heat the apple cider vinegar until the rock sugar has dissolved. Stirring constantly, add the apple, onion, walnut, lemon juice, finely chopped sage, and spices. Boil for fifteen minutes, stirring constantly.

Immediately pour into sterilized glass jars. Close the jar with the original lid. Turn the glass jars upside down and allow them to rest for a while. This makes a wonderful gift to your hostess.

For your child's next birthday party, try this wonderfully refreshing beverage made with apple cider vinegar, mineral water, and fresh berries, such as raspberries, blackberries, currants, and blueberries. Cover the fresh berries with apple cider vinegar and let them rest for a week. Separate the liquid, add the mineral water and sugar to taste.

Apple Cider Vinegar for the Home

To Dissolve Deposits

You can dissolve hard-water deposits in pots by filling the container with water and adding 3 tbs. (45 ml) of apple cider vinegar. Let the mixture sit for several hours. Then, you'll be able to wipe the deposits out easily.

You can spray plants that are infested with lice or other pests with vinegar water to which you've added a little bit of salt.

"Ring around the Collar"

Spray severely soiled laundry with apple cider vinegar before tossing it into the washing machine. Dirt dissolves more easily, and the laundry will be softer.

Cleaning

❖ Soak sponges and brushes in vinegar water (mix 1:1) overnight.
❖ Soak leather cloths used to clean windows in vinegar water (mix 1:1) overnight to keep them soft.
❖ Disinfect and deodorize kitchen cutting boards by scrubbing them with undiluted apple cider vinegar.
❖ Add apple cider vinegar to the last rinse water for woolens, silks, or other delicate fabrics. It works as a fabric softener, and it also brightens colors.
❖ Clean silk lamp shades carefully with lukewarm vinegar water so that the silk material doesn't discolor.
❖ Clean the carpet with a sponge saturated in vinegar water to brighten the colors and remove the spots.

Caring for Flowers

❖ Cut flowers will last longer if you add 2 tbs. (30 ml) of vinegar and 2 tbs. (30 ml) of sugar to the water in the vase.
❖ You can remove the dust from potted plants with wide leaves, such as rubber tree plants, with a lukewarm mixture of apple cider vinegar and water (mix 1:1).

About the Author

Margot Hellmiss has been involved in the field of natural cosmetics, natural healing methods, alternative therapy, and health diets for many years. She is a successful author who has written books offering advice in the area of health.

Note

This book has been carefully edited and produced. Nevertheless, all advice is given without guarantee and neither the author or the publishers can be held liable for any damages that may result from following the practical advice given in this book. Anyone with serious or persistent symptoms should consult a physician.

Photo Credits

AKG, Berlin: 13; Bilderberg, Hamburg: 26 (Klaus Bossemeyer); 91 (Reinhart Wolf); bkp, Berlin: 15; Image Bank, Munich 6 (Nino Mascardi), 9 (Peter Miller), 75 (Gio Barto), 76 (Brigitte Lambert); Kerth, Ulrich, Munich: Cover photo, 80: Mauritius, Mittenwald: 1 (Scheurecker), 18 (Rosenfeld), 42, 85 (AGE), 44 Hubatka; Südwest Verlag, Munich (c): 16; Visum, Hamburg: (Günter Beer)

Index